SPIRITUAL
PRACTICES
for the
BRAIN

SPIRITUAL
PRACTICES
for the
BRAIN

CARING FOR MIND, BODY, AND SOUL

ANNE KERTZ KERNION

LOYOLA PRESS.
A JESUIT MINISTRY
Chicago

LOYOLA PRESS.
A JESUIT MINISTRY

3441 N. Ashland Avenue
Chicago, Illinois 60657
(800) 621-1008
www.loyolapress.com

Scripture quotations are from *New Revised Standard Version Bible: Catholic Edition*, copyright ©
1989, 1993 National Council of the Churches of Christ in the United States of America. Used
by permission. All rights reserved worldwide.

Cover art credit: Illustration by Anne Kertz Kernion. Design by Cheryl Martin.
Interior art credits: Illustrations by Anne Kertz Kernion
Back cover author photo, Jackson Kernion.

ISBN: 978-0-8294-5043-9
Library of Congress Control Number: 2020941382

Printed in the United States of America.
20 21 22 23 24 25 26 27 28 29 Versa 10 9 8 7 6 5 4 3 2 1

In gratitude to my parents,
Joanne and Red Kertz,
for providing me with a happy childhood,
filled with adventure and opportunities.

To Bonnie,
Christmas Blessings
2020!
with hope for healing
in 2021!

Di

CONTENTS

It isn't more light we need, it's putting into practice what light we already have. When we do that, wonderful things will happen within our lives and within our world.

—PEACE PILGRIM

Spirituality is . . . the story of our passionate affair with what is deepest inside us and with the candle that's always flickering inside us and sometimes almost seems to go out and sometimes blazes. And religion is the community, the framework, the tradition, all the other people into which we bring what we find in solitude.

—PICO IYER

FOREWORD

Ar scáth a chéile a mhaireann na daoine.

—IRISH PROVERB

How can we live a more intentionally simple yet abundant life? What difference can we make in our own little corner of the world? How can we raise our children to be kinder, happier, more empathetic, and more peaceful? How can we be at peace despite the trials we undoubtedly will suffer?

These universal questions lie at the heart of humanity, regardless of our level of education, our background, or our faith. They are questions that bind us together in our relationships and our search for God. Anne Kertz Kernion's lovely book reminds me of the Irish proverb "Ar scáth a chéile a mhaireann na daoine," which literally translates as "People live in each other's shadows." We are protected from the sun by one another and rely on others for shelter, goodness, and kindness. Like one plant in a vast garden, each of us has a place in this complex world. What we do affects the whole.

The year 2020 will be written into the history books as a time of unbridled change. The story of this time continues to unfold, full of questions and uncertainty. While not specifically written to address the radical developments of this year, Anne's prophetic work is littered with insights that define the era of change we are living through and will bear witness to. With the advent of the COVID-19 pandemic, the way we live, where we pray, how we grieve, and how we celebrate have all changed. Schools, colleges, and universities sent their students home to be educated there; businesses closed and adapted; public worship was postponed; and we as a people found other ways to shop, pray, live, grieve, celebrate, and grow our communities. This was a time of flux and seeming instability but also a time to slow down, to spend more time inside our homes than in our cars, and to experience more time for introspection and contemplation. For some this time brought rest and healing; for others it brought sadness and anxiety. For all of us it ushered in a season of change.

Anne's words stand at the intersection of a time in history when change rules the roost but offers timeless and new ways of looking at ourselves, our faith, and the wider world. In this delightful book, I encountered new ways of approaching spirituality, neuroscience, and the natural world in a seamless and thoughtful way. Anne is a master at weaving a tapestry of complex thought that comes together in a simple and accessible quilt of ideas stitched together with care.

If you are searching for a place to enter the conversation on spirituality or are a veteran seeking to lean on new insights from the world of science and research, *Spiritual Practices for the Brain* is a book you will savor. You will find that it stands the test of time as it threads the needle on practices old and new that can nourish and energize our faith lives.

Today we are learning anew the power of empathy, the value of vulnerability, and the effects of cultivating emotional intelligence. Anne brings together themes of kindness, empathy, gratitude, and vulnerability-based leadership and does so through Scripture, the lives of the saints, and the extraordinary witness of holy people striving for a more just and thoughtful world—a more truly Christian world. Navigating new ways of being always brings growth, and *Spiritual Practices for the Brain* certainly provides fertile ground to wrestle with the challenge of being a Christian in a post-Christian world. Is this is a book for Catholics? Yes. The Catholic Church has never shied away from difficult but necessary conversations. As a tradition, it has encouraged innovation, questioning, and curiosity, particularly in relation to the arts, science, the written word, and the natural world. Some of the greatest advances the world has ever known have come from inquiring, faithful minds, and Anne has certainly joined the ranks of such inquisitive thinkers.

Is this a book that all Christians can appreciate? Undoubtedly. But it also offers tremendous wisdom for people of all faiths, little faith, and even those who claim to have no faith at all. This is a book I would share with my Lutheran neighbor and my atheist and agnostic friends. With so many of us striving for wholeness and wellness today, this book is a gem and offers a compelling reason for those who have dismissed religion and spirituality to take a second look. Happiness, healthiness, and holiness are linked together, proposes Anne, and she leads the reader on a quest to discover, uncover, and rediscover practices that nourish, strengthen, and uplift.

It is rare for me to read a book in one sitting as a busy mom of three young children, but I found that I could not put this book down. I discovered it to be a comfort but also a challenge, and that is what our Catholic faith invites us to do: to reexamine our old ways of being and shed those ways in light of the call of the Gospel. Since I have read this book, I have dipped in and out of its wellspring many times as I worked through a problem, sought insights, or looked for inspiration.

Not only does Anne link ancient truths with new information and emerging insights, she does so in a way that is practical, accessible, and real. Like a cup of tea or coffee on a damp dreary day, her words delight and invite the reader to consider life afresh. Settle down and settle in for a read that will bring challenge, growth, and renewal for you and all those with whom you share this lovely work.

Beannachtai (Blessings),

Julianne Stanz

INTRODUCTION

Centuries ago, in a world very different from yours and mine, St. John of the Cross (1542–1591) recommended that we "carve out a day every week, or an hour a day, or a moment each hour, and abide in the loving silence of the Friend. Feel the frenetic concerns of life fall away."

Frenetic concerns: now that's a phrase totally relatable to the present time! Perhaps St. John's world was not so different after all.

Another piece of wise advice comes from St. Francis de Sales: "Never be in a hurry; do everything quietly and in a calm spirit. Do not lose your inner peace for anything whatsoever, even if the whole world seems upset. Half an hour's meditation each day is essential, except when you are busy. Then a full hour is needed." He also said this about meditation: "If the heart wanders or is distracted, bring it back to the point quite gently . . . and even if you did nothing during the whole hour but bring your heart back. . . . though it went away every time, your hour would be very well employed."[1]

St. Francis's advice about a wandering heart or a distracted mind could be applied to a class on meditation at your local community center today. It seems that wisdom, whether for the body or the soul, is timeless.

Yet, our world keeps developing as we continue to learn more about the human person. The voice of the divine speaks through the ancient prophets, poets, mystics, and saints, and continues to provide fresh information to discover and explore. In this day and age, much of that information is discovered, interpreted, developed, and applied through the marvelous sciences that have emerged in relatively recent times: biology, psychology, sociology, environmental science, meteorology, molecular biology, and on and on.

No topic is more current or exciting than the recent research on neuroscience and its applications to our everyday lives. And we are finding that neuroscience research, positive psychology studies, and the teachings in our Catholic tradition converge regarding the ways we can flourish as healthy human beings. Several practices that enhance our spiritual lives also bring changes to our brains, nourishing our health down to the cellular level, and amazingly, even affecting how fast we age!

An explosion of studies in recent years investigate spiritual practices and how they benefit our bodies, brains, and emotional well-being. The Christian tradition possesses rich insights that research is now proving enhances not only our spiritual lives but also our health and well-being. Thousands of scientific studies have produced groundbreaking insights due to the power of MRI machines and other investigative tools. In addition, research in the burgeoning field of positive psychology points to several spiritual practices that not only aid our psychological health but also enrich our physical health. These spiritual habits affect us all the way down to the cells in our DNA and our brains.

Additionally, we now understand in greater detail how practices that formerly were seen merely as *spiritual* benefit us as whole people: body, mind, *and* spirit. Our scientific discoveries provide practical means of improving the quality of life—through the spiritual qualities we have valued all along.

What changes occur in our brains when we slow down, live with mindful awareness, serve others, or spend time in nature? How are our brains affected by distraction, over-stimulation, lack of sleep, and the absence

> The notion that science and spirituality are somehow mutually exclusive does a disservice to both.
> —Carl Sagan

of quiet time to ponder the tiny miracles of everyday life? Our technological age, with its ubiquitous devices, makes this last question more important and timely than ever. Everyone who cares about her health and longevity, the vitality of his brain, or her spiritual growth and practices would likely be curious about these discoveries and, more important, how to incorporate them into daily life.

Knowing how to cultivate these practices and why they will improve our health can inspire new habits to help us thrive and flourish on our Christian journey.

St. Teresa of Avila's definition of contemplative prayer is cited in the *Catechism of the Catholic Church*: "Contemplative prayer means . . . taking time frequently to be alone with [God] who we know loves us." The *Catechism* continues, in the section about meditation, by advising: "Christians owe it to themselves to develop the desire to meditate regularly."[2] We hear this guidance in our church documents to nurture a meditation practice, and following this, we can experience the deep, fruitful silence of God's grounding love.

My hope is that you will see the amazing connections between our spiritual practices and our health and well-being. I believe we can become better motivated to develop such practices when we know the scientific basis behind claims of well-being, and when we understand that the implications of this research extend beyond our spiritual lives. For anyone reading this book who is not particularly religious, the science, along with the practices I describe and suggest, can provide non-intimidating ways for you to sample spiritual practices and experience some of their positive effects.

Whether this is your first time hearing about these practices or your twentieth, I hope that the information and stories you read here will motivate you to incorporate a few of these practices into your daily routines. I promise you will be happier and healthier as a result.

> We ought never to fear truth, nor become trapped in our own preconceived ideas, but welcome new scientific discoveries with an attitude of humility.
> —Pope Francis

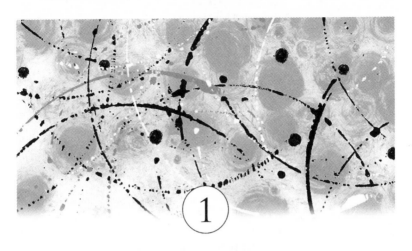

Taking a Breath, Paying Attention

Sometimes the most important thing in a whole day
is the rest we take between two deep breaths.
—Etty Hillesum

We live in a neighborhood at the top of a mile-long hill, and the bottom of the road ends at a busy thoroughfare. The traffic light at this intersection was recently updated with newfangled traffic-control technology. This should be good news, right? Well, it certainly reduced congestion on the main artery, lessening the frequent backups for those travelers. However, the upgrade came with a downside for us, resulting in significantly longer wait times on our end. At first I was disappointed. But then came the realization that these stoppages could be reframed as gifts of time. At the beginning of every drive, I could enjoy several minutes to simply breathe and rest. Breathe and be grateful. Breathe and open my eyes to the beauty around me: the wide expanse of sky above the tree line in the distance, bouquets of wild daisies to my right, and the occasional bird flying above. By reframing these delays as gifts of time, I could turn the inconvenience of a longer wait into a mindful breathing break.

Learning to Breathe

We encounter situations like this regularly: unexpected delays that cause inconveniences. But if we step back and ponder our agitation, we discover its source is in our perspective. Instead of thinking of these moments as wasted, and becoming unsettled by waiting, we can take a breath or two and rest. Etty Hillesum observes that this rest might be the most important thing in our busy day. Our attitudes toward delays can be transformed, allowing gratitude and presence to emerge during wait times. We have an opportunity to rest, breathe deeply, and accept as a gift the minute or two of silence. These little bits of calm and peace are available every single day if we simply remember to view our waiting times as opportunities instead of irritations.

> We need to step aside from the rush of daily life and compose our souls before God, as Jesus did.
> —*United States Catholic Catechism for Adults*, 2006

Hillesum was keenly aware of the fact that our breath is the primary activity connecting us to inner peace in daily life and is the easiest way to be awake to the present moment. When I experienced frustration sitting at our new traffic light for the first time, I remembered to breathe. I could treat those minutes at the traffic light with reverence, as a "sacrament of the present moment," in the words of French Jesuit Father Jean Pierre de Caussade. Caussade wrote that we could seize upon what each unique moment brings.[3] But in our modern, busy lives, we value efficiency and often miss the moment—indeed, often multiple moments. We get to the end of a decade and ask, "Where *was* I in those ten years? They have flown by, and I've hardly remembered to stop and enjoy anything." We may have rushed through our to-do lists, perhaps accomplishing much, without connecting to the profound richness of life. By slowing down and taking a deep breath every once in a while, we remember that we possess this great gift. It's like we have little retreats throughout our days.

PRACTICE: A SIMPLE BREATHING EXERCISE

Find a comfortable place to sit with a tall, straight back. Read the instructions below, then close your eyes and begin.

First, take a deep breath through your nose, if possible. Pause at the end of your inhalation. Now exhale to a count of five. Repeat this four more times. Then open your eyes and continue with your day.

Consciously taking a few breaths grounds us in the moment and illustrates how breathing is a fundamental aspect of spirituality. The word *breath*, or a variation of it, is found in all the major religions, and many of the lesser-known traditions, as well. *Breath* and *spirit* are often translated from the same word. For instance, *spirit* comes from the Latin word *spirare*, meaning "to breathe." *Pneuma* is an ancient Greek word for "breath" and is also translated as "spirit" or "soul." The Hebrew word *ruach* means "breath" or "wind" or "spirit" and is the animating dynamic of creation. *Prana* in Hinduism means "life breath" or "life energy." In Native American traditions, the space between the in-breath and out-breath is considered sacred space. So, when we breathe, we are infusing our lives with Spirit and paying better attention to our basic gift of life.

The simple breathing break can also be a prayer practice by reciting a sacred word or two with each inhalation and exhalation.

> We must remember God more often than we draw breath.
> —St. Gregory of Nazianzus

You can say, "Be still," as you inhale, and "Be at peace," as you exhale. Or recite to yourself, *God's peace*, as you inhale, *Be with me*, as you exhale. Any short phrase can be used to anchor your attention. This is an easy and effective way to bring our focus back to the life we are living right here, right now.

When we hear people say, "I need to take a breather" or "I can't catch my breath" or "My schedule is suffocating," they are indicating their need to pay closer attention to life—by beginning with basic breathing and stillness. The breath is one of the easiest ways to create space even in the busiest of times. When we create that space, we are able to experience the simple joys life offers us. We live in the here and now, not rehashing the past or worrying about the future. This awareness prevents the distraction and numbness resulting from busyness.

It's not surprising that ancient wisdom about breath and being present is confirmed in today's science and discovery. Psychologists Matthew Killingsworth and Daniel Gilbert conducted a huge study with more than fifteen thousand people and 650,000 data points, concluding that almost half the time, subjects were not paying attention to the present moment.[4] Their attention was on the future or on reprocessing a past event. When we live like this, we aren't happy, because our minds aren't here, now. People were happier taking out the trash or doing chores if they were present in the moment than when they were vacationing or attending a party but not living in the moment. Killingsworth and Gilbert concluded that "a wandering mind is an unhappy mind."[5] Their main conclusion is that we must ground ourselves in the present moment to nurture happiness.

Attending to our breath throughout the day is also very helpful to our physical health. Of course, our body systems keep us breathing all day and all night, without our

> The spirit of God has made me, and the breath of the Almighty gives me life.
> —Job 33:4

having to think about it. But to stop and consciously take one breath in, one breath out, focusing just on that breath, is an entirely different experience. We focus just on the many facets of breathing in, pausing, breathing out, pausing, releasing any worries, upsets, or obsessive thoughts. If we pay attention to our breath, we return our minds to the present moment and to the beauty of this day. It is a gift! If I'm feeling angry, or disappointed, or upset, I begin breathing and focus on my exhalations. Focusing on the way we breathe promotes calm by signaling our nervous system to slow our heart rate and digestion, initiating the relaxation response.

What is the relaxation response?[6] It is the opposite of the fight-or-flight response we experience in stressful situations, when our hearts race and our bodies go on high alert. The fight-or-flight response helped our ancestors survive life-threatening situations, but the challenges of modern life don't include (for most of us, anyway) lions and tigers and bears. When we activate this response several times a day, nearly every system of our bodies is affected negatively. Consequently, we're at risk for a host of ailments, including high blood pressure, cardiovascular disease, and accelerated aging. Instead, if we take a few deep breaths when stressful situations occur, we reduce our tension and slow the release of stress hormones such as cortisol. A few mindful breaths also lead to healthier attitudes, increased concentration, healthier immune systems, increased heart rate variability, and more positive emotions. This practice also reduces mind wandering, emotional reactivity, and symptoms associated with anxiety, insomnia, post-traumatic stress disorder, depression, and attention deficit disorder. That's a lot of positives from a simple practice like paying attention to our breath![7]

PRACTICE: ANOTHER SIMPLE BREATH

Set a timer for one minute and count how many breaths you take. Don't change anything in the way you normally breathe. Now remember that number and know that anytime you can take a one-minute pause, you just need to count that number of breaths. It's a handy technique to use in any stressful situation you may encounter, hopefully one that doesn't include bears.

One effective calming-breath technique is to extend exhalations longer than inhalations. When we elongate our outbreath, our heart rate slows. I had the opportunity to practice this on a particularly turbulent flight into Newark, New Jersey. As we were descending through a completely clear sky, the plane unexpectedly began to sway from side to side and bump up and down. I've experienced some rough flights before, but this was one of the worst, in part because it came out of nowhere. My heart began pounding, and I instantly began to consciously breathe: in for four counts, out for six. With each long exhalation, I released a little bit more of the distress. It took several minutes, and by the time I'd calmed down, the turbulence was over.

When we experience a real or imagined emergency situation such as this, we can take control of our breath so that we respond with more calm.

PRACTICE: THE 4–6 BREATH

The 4–6 breath is an excellent tool for slowing our heart rate. When we inhale, our heart rate speeds up. When we exhale, our heart rate decreases, releasing tension and agitation. These extended exhalations suppress the sympathetic nervous system and also stimulate the vagus nerve. This nerve carries information between the brain and other organs, helping to control our bodies' responses when we rest and relax.

To practice the 4–6 breath, count to four as you inhale, then pause. Count to six as you exhale, then pause again. Continue breathing and counting like this for five to ten minutes.

When we pause and take a breath or two, we focus our attention and interrupt any mindless chatter in our brains. These intentional breaths will also boost our brain health. How can a simple exercise accomplish this?

In a recent study, researchers found that the way we breathe affects the chemistry in our brains and can improve our brain health.[8] When we focus on our breath and regulate our breathing, we optimize our attention. This occurs because noradrenaline (also known as norepinephrine), a chemical messenger in the brain, is produced at the ideal level. If we are stressed, we produce too much of this messenger and become mentally scattered, unable to focus properly. If we produce too little, we feel listless, and our attention wanders. There seems to be a precise amount of noradrenaline necessary for us to experience emotional stability and clear thinking. Breath-centered practices appear to provide these benefits.

Noradrenaline also affects our brain mass. Typically, we lose brain matter as we age. But with the right dose of noradrenaline, the brain grows new connections. Researchers believe this may be a reason why the brains of older people who have practiced meditation for many years are more youthful and at less risk of dementia. These meditators boost their neural networks simply by sitting and attending to their breath. That information is sure to boost our motivation to just sit and breathe!

Mindfulness: Glances at God

The practice of breathing and bringing one's mind fully into the present moment is one form of mindfulness. The term *mindfulness* is used in many ways and by many people. The sense of mindfulness I mean is that of bringing attention to the here and now, not worrying about the past or fretting about the future. We are awake to all that life offers us, not rushing from one task to another, unaware of this great gift right in front of us. We refrain from judging our thoughts and behaviors or replaying yesterday's events. We forgo agonizing about the future and all the possible things that might go wrong. In being mindful, we are simply present to the moment God has given us, here and now.

But focusing on the "now" takes commitment and daily practice to make it a habit. We get caught up in our never-ending lists of things to do, and our thoughts wander. But we practice continually bringing our awareness back into the present moment, over and over again, without judgment.

This conscious attentiveness prevents the distraction and numbness that we often feel, which results from too many duties and obligations to fulfill. Prayerful attentiveness refuses to carry the burdens of worry into every single minute of the day.

> "So do not worry about tomorrow, for tomorrow will bring worries of its own. Today's trouble is enough for today."
> —Matthew 6:34

This is one of the simplest ways to experience the joys that life offers each day. We remember that it's amazing we are even here on earth!

Recent research on mindfulness shows that this practice can affect our DNA. Studies have found significant improvements in the subjects' psychological/social well-being, a greater sense of connection, and more awareness in general. Researchers also reported increased activity in areas of the brain related to calm and focus, significantly lower expression of inflammatory genes, and a greater expression of genes boosting immunity. These results were displayed after practicing mindfulness for just twelve weeks.

A Little Glance at God

One of my favorite teachers of Christian mindfulness is Brother Lawrence, a lay brother who lived centuries ago in a Parisian monastery. Lawrence was a cook who dealt with stress from various sources: monotonous tasks, discontent, disorder, and ingratitude from his fellow monks.

> It is possible to offer fervent prayer even while walking in public or strolling alone, or seated in your shop, . . . while buying or selling, . . . or even while cooking.
> —St. John Chrysostom

Tedious kitchen duties aside, he advises us to "get used to offering your heart to God whenever you can." We can offer little glances to God all throughout the day and live in the present moment. The ability to live in the present, with an awareness of God's presence, is not easy to maintain. Brother Lawrence acknowledges that the practice is difficult at first but gradually leads to the awareness that God is always with us, everywhere, without exception. "We can do little things for God," even "flipping my little omelet in the frying pan for the love of God."[9] He believed that the "practice of the presence of God is the essence of the spiritual life."[10]

Another insightful teacher of Christian mindfulness is St. Teresa of Ávila, who remarked, "The Lord walks among the pots and pans."[11] What is it about kitchen duties that inspired both of these luminaries to suggest we can find God there? Perhaps because we can turn those mundane moments of washing and cooking "among the pots and pans" into moments of awareness of the divine presence. Unless you have a cook and a maid, you spend more than a few minutes in the kitchen every day, and instead of racing through those routine tasks to arrive at more interesting ones, we can cultivate mindful silence. I wish I'd been aware of these teachers years ago, when my life had lots and lots of pots and pans.

More recently, Harvard psychology professor Dr. Ronald Siegel discusses the tradition of contemplative prayer in the daily lives of Christians today. Siegel confirms that this type of prayer, including *lectio divina*, the "holy reading" of Scripture, is considered a form of mindfulness practice by secular scholars.[12] This is important news for Christians, because most writers on the topic fail to illuminate Christian forms of mindfulness. In addition, a recent paper noted that "the positive health prospects for mindfulness are pertinent to Christian mindfulness meditation."[13]

Harvard psychologist Ellen Langer provides a slightly different perspective on mindfulness. She recommends that we take time to intentionally notice things, drawing novel distinctions.[14] Noticing the people we live and work with, paying full attention to the subtleties they express, will bring the quality of mindfulness to the day. As we attend to the details of every person and everything around us, we are situated in the present and engaged in life. As we develop this skill of perception, we cultivate mindfulness because we are fully anchored in the present moment.

Bringing our awareness back to the present moment again and again, noticing the details of our surroundings, creates a sense of sacred space and expanded time. Within weeks, the feeling of being pressed for time will slowly dissolve. This is the primary cause of stress: the perceived lack of time. When we practice residing fully in the present, our experience of time is enlarged.

PRACTICE: BRINGING MINDFULNESS TO THE KITCHEN

The next time you are in the kitchen washing dishes, focus all your attention on that task. Feel the warm water on your hands, notice the soapy suds on your fingertips, watch the bubbles disappear as the clear water rinses the dish. Take deep breaths as you use all your senses to fully experience this moment. And give a little glance to God, as Brother Lawrence recommends.

We can also mindfully, prayerfully take a walk. No analyzing, comparing, planning dinner, or ruminating about past conversations with friends or colleagues. Simply notice the various features of nature or the city street. Breathe deeply, and focus your attention on the sights, sounds, and scents all around you.

Finding time throughout the day to practice the art of mindfulness is easy because it doesn't require any additional time or commitment. For many years, I would get anxious if a deadline loomed. Instead of making time, which isn't possible, of course, I wound up wasting it by panicking—becoming stressed about being stressed! When we become more mindful in daily

> We never live. We are always in the expectation of living.
> —Voltaire

life, not only will we will feel better, but also our blood pressure will fall.[15]

PRACTICE: WALKING MINDFULNESS

Walking mindfulness can be practiced anywhere, anytime. Find a trail outdoors or a room indoors. Even a long hallway at work or school will suffice. You can use a small room in your home, since this practice doesn't require a large space. I sometimes walk around the edges of a six-by-nine-foot area rug.

When walking, focus on each little movement: Lift your foot off the ground, bring it forward, then place the heel of your foot on the floor. Now shift your body weight onto your forward foot and leg. Begin lifting the heel of your back foot. Raise that foot off the ground, aware of each movement of lifting: first the heel, then the middle of your foot, then peeling your toes up off the ground. Bring that foot forward, and now that heel comes to the ground as your weight shifts again to your forward foot. This process should be done slowly and mindfully. When your thoughts wander, as they will, simply acknowledge them and bring your attention back to each small movement of your feet.

You can link your fingers behind your back or let your arms hang by your side, whatever feels most comfortable to you. As you walk, focus attention on the breath as you inhale or exhale, or focus on the area right in front of your foot. You can also simply attend to the movements of your feet, arms, torso, and legs, maybe even imagine breathing in God's peace with every step.

Mindful people embody the quality of graciousness, which is not cultivated when we are pressed for time. Mindful folks live with a sense of ease and grace, even in the face of adversity. As a frequent flyer, I often witness airline passengers who are confronted with adversity in the guise of long delays or canceled flights. Reactions to disrupted plans range from mild annoyance to explosive anger. It's fascinating to observe when gracious passengers, with calm and self-restraint, bring their travel predicament to the gate agent. With patience and grace, such people model for the rest of us how to handle annoyance with poise. Their attitudes are gifts to all of us and lift my spirits as well as others', I'm sure.

PRACTICE

This week, look for signs of graciousness in others. Perhaps offer your gratitude, so they know their patience is appreciated. Also this week, practice being gracious when life gets difficult. Refrain from expressing your impatience and frustration. Then notice how much better you feel.

Here are four mindfulness practices we can easily assimilate into our days.

PRACTICE

1. **Mindful eating.** Many of our social activities revolve around food, so eating mindfully isn't always possible. But we can frequently take time to bring our full awareness to every detail as we eat. What colors are in the food? How does it smell? What are its shapes? Ponder those small details; then bring the food to your mouth and chew slowly. Take note of how the food feels in your mouth and on your tongue. How does it taste? Observe every detail as you swallow and prepare to take another bite. Afterward, sit quietly and perhaps say a short prayer of thanks for the wondrous gift of digestion.
2. **Mindful tea or coffee ritual.** Every morning, I grind coffee beans, boil water, pour it over the ground beans and warm cream for my coffee. I also soak a tea bag in a mug for my husband, then add a bit of sugar to each serving. This mindful ritual begins my day slowly, with a gentle awareness. You might focus on your hand movements as you grind coffee or pour water for tea. Take a moment to smell the beans, the tea, or the brewed coffee. No rushing at all. It's a beautiful way to begin the day.

3. **Mindful waiting.** In the words of Ralph Waldo Emerson, "How much of human life is lost in waiting?" We are a society that seems to have lost the ability to wait for anything. We notice people texting at stoplights and checking their phones in line at the bank or grocery store. A few minutes before (and even during!) a sporting or cultural event is to begin, we see folks scrolling through their phones for entertainment or information. What if we put down our phones and just looked around? We could even strike up a conversation with someone. Everyone has something to teach us, if we just have ears to listen. What if we viewed each moment of waiting as a gift?

4. **Mindful driving.** Of course, we should be mindful when we drive! But if we're honest, that's not always the case. Unless we're just learning to drive, it becomes automatic to us. So we turn on the radio and listen to music or news, play a podcast, think about the day's meetings and obligations, or plan weekend activities. Next time you're in the car, try to bring full awareness to the *experience* of driving. Notice how the steering wheel feels in your hands and how the seat cushion supports you. Simply observe the sky, other cars, the buildings that pass by, perhaps the trees and flowers and vegetation along the way. Turn off the radio or your phone, and refrain from getting lost in thoughts not related to driving. Just notice and be aware, mindful of the gift of modern transportation.

With practice, we can create a sense of sacred space in whatever we do. All that is necessary is bringing full awareness to the present task.

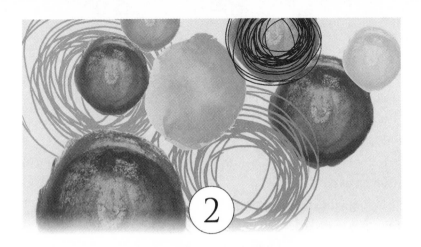

2

UNDERSTANDING MEDITATION

Do not worry about your life. . . . Can any one of you by worrying
add a single hour to your span of life?
—MATTHEW 6:25–27

In our fast and overscheduled lives, we recognize the need to slow down and be present to our lives as they unfold before us. But many Catholics and other Christians are completely unaware of contemplative teachings, rooted in the church's history, that can help us nurture silence. These teachings, beginning with luminaries such as the Desert Fathers and Mothers from the third century, are deep depositories of wisdom for the modern, often harried, person. The desert hermits of the early Christian church sought to live in the presence of God by retreating to the solitude of the desert and practicing what was known as the prayer of quiet, developing a purity of heart. They found that this practice nurtured both their spiritual lives and their psychological health. Later, between the twelfth and seventeenth centuries, several Christian figures further developed the theological and practical underpinnings of this practice, including Francis de Sales; the mystics Julian of Norwich, Teresa of Ávila, John of the Cross; and the anonymous author of *The Cloud of Unknowing*. Julian of Norwich reminds us that the best prayer is to "rest in the goodness of God, for that goodness reaches to the depths of our needs." Her most famous line, "All shall be well . . ." continues on, as she notes "for there is a Force of love moving through the universe that holds us fast and will never let us go."

Sitting in silence is not easy, as Brother Lawrence remarked: "You are not the only one who experiences distractions . . . Strive to be attentive to God's presence. If your mind wanders or withdraws occasionally, don't get upset."[16] Francis de Sales advises us to keep bringing our hearts back, regardless of the inevitable distractions. These instructions are particularly relevant, because the chief objection I hear about committing to meditation is this: "I'm just not good at this. My mind keeps racing the whole time." Guess what? Join the club! That's what our human minds do. They jump around from one thing to the next as soon as we sit down. But like any skill, meditation takes time and practice. A lot of it. Ever so slowly, you'll come to the point where you can sit, focus on a sacred word or your breath, and gently let go of thoughts over and over again. A wandering mind simply presents more opportunities to come back to center, to the simple awareness of this gift of life and of God's presence. Over and over and over again. The more we practice, the more returning to God becomes a habit.

> We need silence to be able to touch souls.
> —St. Teresa of Calcutta

In the mid-twentieth century, the Cistercian monk Thomas Merton recovered the teachings of these desert hermits and mystics for the benefit of modern-day Christians. Merton stressed that solitude and silent prayer were essential to living a Christian life.[17] He observed that contemplation cultivates an openness to life, a deep attentiveness, and a reverence for the world around us. If we live with this contemplative attitude, we will be filled with joy. "Contemplation is the highest expression of intellectual and spiritual life. It is that life itself, fully awake, fully active, fully aware that it is alive. It is spiritual wonder. It is spontaneous awe at the sacredness of life, of being. It is gratitude for life, for awareness and for being."[18]

PRACTICE: SACRED WORD

1. **Sit in a quiet space, with your back straight and feet on the ground.** Close your eyes and pay attention to your breathing. Perhaps set a timer for five or ten minutes.

2. **Choose a sacred word on which to focus your attention.** Examples you might consider are *Jesus, peace, love, stillness,* or *mercy*.

3. **When a thought arises, as it surely will, gently guide your attention back to your sacred word.** Let go of all judgment and disappointment. Every time you return is an opportunity to strengthen your focusing muscles and your attention on God's presence. Continue until the timer sounds.

4. **When the time is up, stay sitting and take a few deep breaths of thanksgiving.** Open your eyes and return to your daily activities, with a deeper awareness of God and of others.

I was sweeping the floor before exercise class on Saturday morning when one of my students arrived early and we began chatting. Pushing the broom back and forth across the room, I asked Joyce how life had been treating her lately. She sighed and said,

> Leave your front door and your back door open. Allow your thoughts to come and go. Just don't serve them tea.
>
> —Shunryu Suzuki

"Good . . . except that I worry too much. I wish I could stop. Even at the end of class when we just rest, my mind jumps all around. I don't know how to stop it." I took that as an opening to share a helpful exercise.

"Next time you're caught in worry," I said, "picture yourself on the bank of a river, watching boats go by, and think of your thoughts as if they were the boats. As one appears, notice it, maybe even name it ('worry,' 'fear,' 'planning,'), then let it go down the river." Over and over again, "Try not to jump into a boat and ride it down the river. If you find you've become lost in thought, just come back to the river's edge." It's that simple, although it's not necessarily easy. I assured her that if she practiced regularly, she would become more aware of her worrisome thoughts and would be able to catch herself from spiraling into hours of ruminating.

As we practice letting go of thoughts when settling down to pray and meditate, we learn to let go of worry in daily life. It's like practicing anything else. At first, we're not very skilled, but we get better the more we practice. Why do we worry so much to begin with? Because our brains have been trained, from experience and evolution, to amplify the negatives and minimize the positives. This is known as the "negativity bias," which allowed our ancestors to survive in the forest and fields. They needed to be constantly vigilant, asking themselves, *Will that berry poison me?* or *Is that a friendly cat or a mountain lion looking for its next meal?* These were life-or-death questions, and focusing on danger was essential to our ancestors' survival. Today we still must be alert but to different dangers. Most of us don't need to watch out for poison berries or wild animals, but our lives depend on defensive driving and avoiding having our bank accounts hacked. This mental habit, with our brains clinging to bad news like Velcro and good news sliding away as if riding on Teflon, is not helpful. We often quickly react to anything difficult or unpleasant and perhaps start worrying and extrapolating out to the very worst outcome imaginable. (Oh, I've been there, too!) But this tendency destroys our ability to find joy in the moment. Of course, we might not be able to stop worrying completely, but we can learn to notice it, pause, and guide ourselves back to the present moment, to the ease and joy and spaciousness we can find there.

Many of us suffer with overactive minds. And that's why I'm a big cheerleader for meditation. As we practice letting go of thoughts during the time we sit in stillness, we learn to let go of worry when we get out of our chairs and return to daily life.

Being faithful to a meditation practice, "retreating to the desert" each day, provides many lessons, including the practice of allowing stressful situations to play themselves out. If a problem comes up in work or at a conference, I try to take a few deep breaths and remind myself that the world will not end if the issue cannot be resolved. For example, I was leading a catechist retreat one Saturday, and the technology was not cooperating. My presentation was to begin at 9:00 a.m., and for thirty minutes beforehand, the tech folks struggled to get the projector working. I reminded myself not to panic, because really, how was that going to help? Would getting anxious and upset make the problem vanish? Of course not. But it might make the technicians nervous and wouldn't model the behavior I would soon be recommending in my talk. So I simply walked around the area, slowly and contemplatively, taking some deep breaths, waiting for the experts to fix the problem. Luckily, with one minute to go, at 8:59, they found a way for the presentation to display properly. Wasn't it better that I had focused on compassion for them and their discomfort instead of judging them negatively? Thomas Merton observed that cultivating silence and solitude often results in a greater sense of connectedness with others and "leads us back into life, into the arms of the world."[19] Our empathy for and awareness of others become heightened.

> We pray with closed doors when with closed lips and complete silence we pray to the searcher not of words but of hearts.
> —St. John Cassian

Following Merton's untimely death in 1968, a worldwide organization, Contemplative Outreach, was launched to teach a form of meditation called centering prayer.

> Frequently, only silence can express my prayer.
> —St. Therese of Lisieux

This contemplative practice is drawn from the writings of the Christian desert hermits and the methods described in the fourteenth-century work *The Cloud of Unknowing*. The primary practice of centering prayer is to sit quietly and repeat a sacred word or phrase. When your attention wanders, return your focus to the word, without judging yourself or reacting negatively to the process. This method, like secular mindfulness meditation, trains the mind to focus and let go of distractions and is exactly the kind of practice recommended to enhance our cognitive abilities.[20] The main difference between secular meditation and Christian meditation is that the latter is about cultivating a relationship with God and resting in that presence.

Two of the best teachers of Christian meditation are James Finley and Fr. Laurence Freeman. Finley explains that Christian meditation can enrich our daily lives by connecting us with the present moment. He describes how to focus our attention and breathing and how to practice walking meditation, compassion, and forgiveness. He shows that all these practices enable the Christian to experience the divine in everyday life. Finley also notes that each of us needs to discover our unique ways to meditate. Whatever nurtures within us a meditative awareness of the present moment can be a meditative experience, like "baking bread, tending the roses, or taking long, slow walks to no place in particular . . . painting . . . reading or writing poetry."[21] When we give ourselves over to these simple activities, we are taken to a deep place where we recognize the face of the divine in every person and everything around us.[22]

Dr. Richard Davidson of the University of Wisconsin is a leading researcher on contemplative practices and neuroscience, studying how meditation affects the brain. He cites the Desert Fathers and Thomas

> Almost everything will work again if you unplug it for a few minutes . . . including you.
>
> —Anne Lamott

Merton in his work, noting that Desert Father Abba Dorotheus said, "Everything you do, be it great or small, is but one-eighth of the problem, whereas to keep one's state undisturbed even if thereby one should fail to accomplish the task, is the other seven-eighths."[23]

Stress, Telomeres, and Our Health

Stress and worry are common maladies in our world today.

Small doses of stress are not problematic. In fact, short-term stressors can be good for us, building our coping skills and resilience muscles. Stress is also helpful if we need an extra burst of energy or concentrated focus. For example, if we witness an accident and need immediate help, we jump into action and adrenaline helps fuel our quick response. It's the long-term stress levels that are the real culprits. Chronic stress, such as worries about work or family issues that linger for months or years, is not beneficial to our health. This type of stress affects our *telomeres*, the protective end caps on our chromosomes, which are analogous to the plastic ends of shoelaces. (These are called aglets, in case you want to impress your friends.) As we age, our telomeres naturally shorten, and that shortening ages us. When skin cells die, we see wrinkles. Hair pigment cells die, and we see gray hair. Shortened telomeres bring about weakened immune systems, heart and lung disease, aging skin and hair, and cognitive slowing.[24] A Dallas study in *JAMA Neurology*, October, 2014, concluded that short telomeres in the blood also indicate an aging brain.[25]

Dr. Elizabeth Blackburn won the 2009 Nobel Prize for her work on telomerase, the enzyme that makes and replenishes our telomeres.

She notes that chronic stress decreases the activity of telomerase, causing our telomeres to shorten. In most of our cells, telomerase generally becomes less active as we age, but stress accelerates the process, resulting in premature aging and a whole host of health-related issues. Old cells secrete proteins, lipids, and other substances that increase inflammation and tissue destruction and also cause damage to key areas of the brain.[26] The good news is that multiple research studies indicate we can increase telomerase naturally to slow, prevent, or even reverse any overshortening of telomeres. Keeping stress at bay through our silent prayer practices will help us maintain healthy telomerase levels.

We might also think about how we allow stress to affect us. Sometimes, even before a stressful event occurs, we begin to get anxious about the difficulties ahead. For example, we might think about an awkward conversation we need to initiate. As we imagine it in our minds, we feel our heart rate rise, our blood pressure go up, and we may begin to sweat. Simply pondering that conversation qualifies as a stressful event, even though the event is occurring only in our mind. But we can change our reactions to mental stressors like this through a meditation practice. As we meditate, we become more aware of our thoughts, including anxious ones, and learn to let them go, over and over again. The more we practice, the more our reactions to stressful thoughts and situations become less dramatic, allowing us to find more calm in our day. Meditation triggers the "relaxation response," a state of rest that decreases stress, heart rate, blood pressure, and alleviates chronic disease symptoms. As a bonus, we will keep our telomeres healthy in the process.

In fact, one research study found that just twelve minutes of meditation a day for two months improved the subjects' telomere maintenance capacity.[27] And in case you're wondering if there's a telomerase drink or pill we can safely ingest, the answer is no, because cancer can result from an oversupply. Incorporating practices such as mindfulness and meditation will help maintain our telomerase levels without any health risks.

I spend many hours in airports, and there is no better preparation for delays, bad weather, and last-minute cancellations than a meditation practice. Letting go of thoughts, one after another after another, trains my mind to stay calm amidst unexpected difficulties. My expectations of arriving on time at my destination can be released, replaced by gratefulness for the gift of life. I can take a leisurely walk around the terminal, people watch, or browse the magazines in the newsstand. I do my best to keep a balanced perspective, pausing to be grateful to the workers who keep air travel safe. As a fellow passenger once commented, "It's better to find a problem while we're on the ground instead of in the air."

PRACTICE: REPLACE ANXIETY WITH BREATHING

Take a moment to close your eyes and breathe. Remind yourself that you are in God's loving presence, enjoying the gift of life and breath. Then count "one" as you breathe in, and "one" as you breathe out. In and out, two. In and out, three. Continue up to ten, then start over. If you get lost before "ten," simply return to "one" and begin again. Remember that this isn't a contest, and there will be no blue ribbons awarded for your performance. Just stay with this for several minutes. Then open your eyes. You've just been nourished by the gift of breath.

The Brain and Meditation

Studies from the University of British Columbia and Harvard have proven that meditation is more than just a relaxation tool that keeps stress at bay. It can also have life-altering effects on your brain. How can a simple meditation exercise, like mindfully watching our breath, support our brain health? There are several ways it accomplishes this. It improves working memory, increases gray matter in the brain, and lessens inflammation and cortisol levels. A 2013 review of three studies suggests that meditation may slow, stall, or even reverse changes that take place in the brain due to normal aging. In addition, improvements in working memory, attention and focus, and less mind-wandering have been documented after just two weeks of meditation.[28] "Evidence has accrued that meditation techniques improve cognitive control, including sustained attention, speed of processing, and working memory capacity."[29]

You might ask what exactly changes in the brain? First, those who practice meditation for many years have more folds in the outer layer of the brain. This process, called gyrification, may increase the brain's ability to process information. Results from a 2012 study funded by the NCCIH (National Center for Complementary and Integrative Health) shows that meditation affects activity in the amygdala by shrinking it. The amygdala is our fight-or-flight center, responsible for processing anxiety and negative emotions. It grows under stress and when activated, increases the strain on our heart and blood vessels, Two-thirds of our amygdala cells track unpleasant experiences. Meditation seems to cause the connections between the amygdala and the rest of the brain to become weaker, while those between the areas associated with attention and concentration get stronger.[30]

Another great side effect of meditation is a reduction in perceived pain and pain-related anxiety with as little as three days of twenty-minute meditation sessions. Meditators feel pain but don't get upset by it. They anticipate pain less, and their pain isn't magnified.

Research also indicates that meditators show increased gray matter and cortical thickness in areas that involve self-regulation and attention conflicts. The prefrontal cortex, responsible for functions such as planning, problem solving, and emotion regulation, is enhanced as well. Lastly, meditation has an effect on the hippocampus, site of memory control and behavioral regulation. The hippocampus is extraordinarily susceptible to stress and stress-related disorders like depression, anxiety, and post-traumatic stress disorders. Stress reduction in general, and meditation in particular, has been shown to substantially expand the volume of the hippocampus.

Meditation also quiets the default mode network in the brain, the area associated with self-related thinking and mind wandering.[31] This means that we are able to step back and become more accepting and grateful, less judgmental and reactive. When we find ourselves in difficult situations, we train our brains to consider our response to the stress calmly instead of quickly reacting in a way we might later regret. The more we practice acting in this way, the more our brains begin to be reshaped by this behavior.

PRACTICE: BELLY BREATHING TO COUNTERACT STRESS

When you feel stressed, sit with one hand on your chest and one on your belly. As you breathe in and out, the hand on your chest should stay still and the hand on your belly should puff out like you're inflating a balloon. This type of belly breathing will interrupt the flight-or-fight response.

Try breathing like this once every hour, and you'll be able to use this tool to thwart an overreaction to stressful events.

A British study published in June of 2017 analyzed eighteen investigations on the biological effects of meditation and breathing practices, among others. These appear to suppress the expression of genes that promote inflammation and to reverse the molecular effects of chronic

I've had a lot of worries in my life, most of which never happened.
—attributed to various people

stress. Meditation has also been found to increase activity in an area of the brain that helps make the immune system act more efficiently and produces more defense cells. Volunteers in one study (University of Wisconsin) who meditated had significantly higher levels of these healthful antibodies than non-meditators after just one to two months. They concluded that a meditation habit can strengthen the body's immune response as well as increase brain performance due to greater neural connectivity.[32]

One might ask if there is a minimum amount of time needed for meditators to achieve quantifiable benefits. Some research indicates that "8 but not 4 weeks of brief, daily meditation . . . enhanced attention, working memory, and recognition memory."[33] This study concluded that just thirteen minutes of daily meditation over eight weeks has a recognizable effect on novice meditators.

One of the most basic meditation practices is the simple act of sitting and breathing, noticing one's breath or repeating a sacred word. Other practices might include walking a labyrinth, baking bread, saying the Rosary, taking a slow nature walk, or perhaps chanting at a Taizé prayer service. Any practice that brings our full attention to the present moment could qualify as a meditative practice. As Fr. Don Grayston said, "Anything that slows us down is a spiritual practice."

I hope you're convinced to try one of the forms of meditation I've discussed. If you don't think you have time to meditate, simply start with two minutes a day. Every one of us can find two minutes to sit and breathe in God's presence. Set your alarm for two minutes earlier than usual. The night before, arrange a chair, blanket, candle, prayer book, or whatever inspires you to begin. Resolve to meditate for a week for just a few minutes, then perhaps add a minute the following week. Make it a daily habit and try not to skip a day. It's more important to meditate frequently than to worry about how long you sit there. Aim for twelve minutes, since research shows that's the minimum length required to see results. Studies also seem to indicate that it's more helpful to sit ten minutes every day of the week than seventy minutes on one day. Start slowly and build. And remember to be gentle with yourself.

One of the reasons that meditation is now being touted in mainstream media is that it confers several remarkable benefits for our brains and bodies. Our cognitive control, attention, processing speed, and working memory are functions that decline as we get older because of the loss of white matter in the brain.[34] But neuroscience research indicates that if we practice meditation on a regular basis, for as little as twelve minutes per day, these processes can be maintained. Dr. Sara Lazar of Harvard found preliminary evidence suggesting that meditation can offset several age-related cognitive declines.[35] In addition, several studies show that meditation may reduce the risk and delay the onset of Alzheimer's disease.[36]

Studies like this could provide motivation to make meditation a habit.

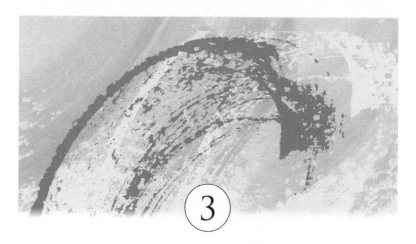

3

LIVING WITH GRATITUDE

It is not joy that makes us grateful.
It is gratitude that makes us joyful.
—BROTHER DAVID STEINDL-RAST

I graduated from Penn State in March of 1981 without any idea how sick I was. My daily runs had been labored since September, after I fainted on the ramp going into the opening day football game. The next day, my fever was so high that my alarmed roommate, Teri, insisted I go to the student infirmary. A week of observation and tests turned up nothing unusual, so they sent me home. I still remember that painfully slow walk back to my apartment, so weak that each step took every ounce of concentration. After finally reaching my apartment, I climbed back into bed and rested for several more days. I regained enough energy to begin attending my final engineering classes, where senior-level coursework would pile up quickly. I eventually got back into a groove of sorts but never shook the exhaustion. I just chalked it up to lingering effects of whatever mysterious illness I had contracted.

Soon after returning to St. Louis after graduation, I fainted in my parents' kitchen while fetching a glass of water at midnight. After being rushed to a nearby hospital and having several rounds of blood tests, we learned that I had toxic shock syndrome (which, it turned out, I'd never fully recovered from since September), with severe anemia as well. But I was really lucky. Many of the reported cases of TSS that year ended in death, and I was fortunate to survive without any serious or long-term side effects.

A few weeks after coming home from the hospital, I was diagnosed with mononucleosis. Now recovering from three major illnesses, physically and mentally exhausted, I slept eighteen hours a day, crawling out of bed every afternoon to eat a small meal and visit with family and friends. The healing process took months, and I vowed that if I ever made a full recovery, I would take good care of my body and never, ever, take my health for granted.

Before this episode, I'd never thought about being grateful for disease-free days. But for a long time after recovery, I counted my blessings every single day. Although I'd had the typical childhood diseases and sports injuries, I'd sprung back quickly, never convalescing for more than a week or two. The tenuous nature of life was front and center, particularly after reading about other young women who hadn't survived toxic shock. These illnesses made me so much more aware of life's gifts. Internalizing how close I'd come to dying brought everything into focus.

Some time after this experience, I came across these words by David Whyte:

> Gratitude is the understanding that many millions of things come together and live together and mesh together and breathe together in order for us to take even one more breath of air, that the underlying gift of life and incarnation as a living, participating human being is a privilege; that we are miraculously part of something rather than

nothing. Even if that something is temporarily pain or despair, we inhabit a living world, with real faces, real voices, laughter, the color blue, the green of the fields, the freshness of a cold wind, or the tawny hue of a winter landscape.

They encapsulate what I began to understand so deeply all those years ago: we are miraculously here, a part of something, and life is a privilege.

PRACTICE

Ponder a few of the ordinary gifts you take for granted: your family, health, friends, house, job, food, etc. Maybe write one or more on a piece of paper or a sticky note. Imagine what life would be like without just one of them. Take a moment to acknowledge your thankfulness. Breathe in gratitude.

Why isn't gratitude second nature to all of us? One reason, as noted earlier, is that our ancestors' brains developed to survive. Their brains were, and now ours are,

> Give thanks in all circumstances.
> —1 Thessalonians 5:18

exceedingly good at finding and holding on to any information that could spell trouble. The practice of gratefulness can help thwart this tendency. Instead of focusing on problems and ignoring all the "good stuff," we can focus on the positive, be grateful for those gifts, and bring more joy into our lives.

Robert Emmons is a psychology professor at University of California, Davis, and a leading expert on the science of gratitude. He defines gratitude as having two main features. First, it is an affirmation of goodness, recognizing that although we have difficulties, gratitude reveals the abundance of goodness right in front of us. Second, we recognize that this goodness, with blessings both big (I landed a wonderful new job!) and small (The dinner last night was delicious.) has been given to us without our earning it.

The key to fostering an attitude of gratitude is to practice it regularly. I'll share some research-based suggestions to help you get started.

1. **Keep a gratitude journal.** Recall all the gifts that have come your way. It's fun to read it later and savor those moments once again. Don't feel that you need to write every day. Instead, try jotting down three things you're grateful for every Sunday. That way, you'll be on the lookout for gifts throughout the week but won't feel the burden of recording them daily.

2. **Seek out prayers of gratitude.** They are powerful sources of inspiration. There are powerful sources of inspiration, such as Psalms (23, 34, 103, 118, 136), online sources (https://www.beliefnet.com/prayers/christian/gratitude/prayer-of-thanksgiving.aspx), and any number of devotional books on the market.

3. **Use your senses—taste, sight, touch, smell, and hearing—to appreciate the miracle of being alive.** You might want to choose one sense each day, or one each week, and focus on the gifts you experience through that particular lens. To nurture my sense of smell, I add a few drops of essential oil to a cotton ball and place it in my workspace or my hotel room. I take a few deep breaths once in a while to enjoy the natural scents. We also have daily opportunities to bring our attention to taste. How many times have we finished a meal and don't remember what it tasted like? It might help to recall how much you appreciate your sense of taste after weathering a bad cold. Try bringing that feeling of gratitude and awareness into your next mealtime, or even into your next bite of chocolate. Who doesn't appreciate a taste

of quality chocolate? It's so easy to miss many of these everyday gifts if we are too busy, rushing from one thing to another.

4. **Set up visual reminders.** I place rocks and stones from our travels in every room to remind myself to be grateful, not only for the vacation spots, but also for the variety and beauty of rock formations on earth. Posting gratitude quotes on your computer or bathroom mirror is another option, or displaying pictures of places and people who are especially dear to you. A simple plaque in my office, a gift from my coworkers, says, "Begin each day with a grateful heart." It's a great reminder at the beginning of each workday.

5. **Smile, look people in the eye, and say thank you.** Write thank-you notes and letters. Seize every opportunity to express your gratitude to others. This practice will bring joy to you and appreciation to others, and the effects can ripple out to many more.

6. **Create a gratitude jar.** Take a few moments every day, or just a few times each week, to write down the blessings that have come your way. They can be big or small. If you have a family, bring everyone into the act. Children who cannot write yet can draw a picture of something they are thankful for. Read the notes at a family dinner to spread an "attitude of gratitude" to all those around the table.

When we celebrate the present by savoring positive experiences, we keep *hedonic adaptation* at bay. Hedonic adaptation is the technical term for what happens when we quickly adjust to a new situation, good or

> When asked if my cup is half-full or half-empty my only response is that I am thankful I have a cup.
> —Sam Lefkowitz

bad. A new "normal" sets in, and appreciation and excitement, or sadness and disappointment, wear off. By practicing gratitude, however, we can magnify positive emotions and halt the tendency to take new circumstances for granted. We celebrate the goodness instead of merely adapting to it. Think about how happy and excited we might be to purchase a new car. From the time we drive it off the lot, to every time we open the door, we can remember how wonderful it is to own this modern form of transportation. Even when the new-car smell dissipates, we continue being grateful, never taking the vehicle for granted. I can be as grateful for my thirteen-year-old car today as I was on the day we bought it. It may not be shiny and new and may have dents and bruises, but it's still reliable and convenient, a gift many in the world wish they had. The more we practice gratitude in this way, the more our brains will scan for the positive. We actually strengthen the neural pathways of gratitude in our brains. Research shows that we'll train our prefrontal cortex (the area of our brain behind the forehead that controls decision making, goal setting, and judgment) to hold on to these positive experiences and deflect negative ones. We solidify the good, and gratefulness becomes a habit ingrained in daily life.

By focusing on the positive in this way, we keep negative emotions such as envy, resentment, and regret—emotions that can destroy our happiness—at bay. Several recent studies show that gratitude can be effective even in treating depression. A 2009 National Institutes of Health (NIH) study showed increased activity in the hypothalamus when we feel gratitude.[37] It is also addictive—another one of the benefits that gratitude research has discovered. When we feel grateful, our brains are flooded with the chemical dopamine, a feel-good hormone. Because of this natural high, we are more inclined to give thanks again and again and again. We can see why grateful people, in general, are happier, more satisfied with their lives, and less likely to suffer from burnout.

Gratefulness will also inhibit the tendency to compare ourselves to others and will thwart perfectionism. When we unthinkingly judge all day long, with likes and dislikes parading through our minds continuously, our relationships suffer. A judgmental attitude helped our ancestors navigate the wild, as they evaluated what would help them stay alive and what might kill them. But constantly judging and critiquing is not beneficial to our well-being in the modern world. On the contrary, it ramps up our stress levels and creates separation from others.

Gratitude helps us become more resistant to stressors. Research concludes that if we have a grateful outlook, then we'll recover more quickly from difficult life events, and we'll lessen our anxiety. "Cultivating appreciation and other positive emotions showed lower levels of stress hormones [specifically] a 23 percent reduction in cortisol and 100 percent increase in DHEA/DHEAS levels."[38] Interestingly, another study found that subjects' heart rates and amygdala activity decreased after gratitude interventions, meaning that emotional regulation improved.[39]

Grateful people also have a higher sense of self-worth. We can notice and thank all the people who are looking out for us, who have helped us get to where we are today. And that makes us feel loved and good about ourselves.

You might wonder what *prevents* us from being grateful. The number-one cause is time scarcity. Research shows that those who are hurried are less grateful, less generous, and less compassionate. So, it's important to be aware of constantly being "too busy." It will thwart your desire to practice an attitude of gratitude.

> The most fortunate are those who have a wonderful capacity to appreciate again and again, freshly and naively, the basic goods of life, with awe, pleasure, wonder and even ecstasy.
> —Abraham H. Maslow

Let's look at some other mental and physical effects of gratitude.

1. **Gratitude makes you more likely to exercise.** According to the *Journal of Personality and Social Psychology*, people who keep

gratitude journals reported fewer health complaints, spent more time exercising, and had fewer symptoms of physical illness.[40]

2. **Gratitude improves the quality of your sleep.** According to a study conducted at the University of Manchester and published in the *Journal of Psychosomatic Research*, regularly focusing on gratitude and thankfulness improved quality of sleep and resulted in longer sleep hours.[41]

3. **Gratitude increases your emotional well-being.** According to studies published in the *Journal of Research in Personality*, gratitude leads to lower depression and higher levels of social support while making you less likely to consider suicide.

4. **Gratitude makes your heart stronger and healthier.** Research conducted at Massachusetts General Hospital found that the presence of gratitude in a patient "may independently predict superior cardiovascular health."[42] Other researchers find that a regular gratitude practice helps lower inflammation and blood pressure, producing calm by activating the parasympathetic system, increasing resilience to disease and trauma, and helping maintain cardiac health.[43] Gratitude also increases the recovery time for heart patients while reducing their inflammatory biomarkers.

5. **Gratitude makes you a more effective leader.** According to a Wharton study, business leaders who practice gratitude have employees who feel more valued, have higher job satisfaction, are motivated to do their best, and have better work relationships. Feeling grateful also increases our desire to persevere toward future goals.[44]

PRACTICE

Tap into gratitude all day simply by asking yourself, *What can I feel grateful for right now, right here?* Brother David Steindl-Rast, the renowned teacher of gratefulness, recommends using the alphabet to help you count your blessings: Start with the letter *A*, and then move to each letter of the alphabet, naming as many things you're grateful for that begin with that letter. Work your way through the alphabet. It may take you twenty-six days, but your gratitude well will be full!

It is especially helpful to practice gratitude when difficulties arise. My coworker and friend Marianne broke her foot last year. It was one of those "don't ask me how it happened" sort of accidents: hanging curtains in her dining room. Instead of moping around, bemoaning the loss of six weeks of driving, walking, and exercise, she began counting all the ways she was grateful:

- She was able to continue performing her work duties.

- Her neighbors and friends were happy to drive her to appointments and errands, and she was glad to spend some extra time with them.

- She didn't injure her arm, which would have been even more inconvenient.

- The injury occurred in the springtime instead of during the holidays or summertime.

- It didn't happen to others in her life who would find the injury much more burdensome.

- Her husband took on new responsibilities, which provided an opportunity for him to learn new skills.

Marianne is a textbook case of how to stave off the blues when things don't go as planned. She is finding things to be grateful for *in* her situation, although she's not grateful *for* her situation. Her "attitude of gratitude" illustrates how this spiritual practice buffered against the stress and negativity her situation might have caused. She was able to count her blessings instead of tallying what went wrong.

Each of us gets knocked around by life now and again, so it's helpful to remember that practicing gratitude can help us cope while also supporting our physical, mental, and spiritual health. Steeped in the power of gratitude, we can be thankful that we simply woke up this morning. This kind of gratitude transforms us, and we then live from a deep well of thanksgiving that will never run dry.

In the end, we understand that cultivating and practicing gratefulness is a *very* different way to live, because it flies in the face of all the messages telling us we need to have more and be more in order to be happy. When we *live* gratitude, we steep ourselves in the power of gratefulness that permeates every moment. This is not just a "something good happened" gratitude or "I got what I wanted" gratitude but an "I woke up again today" and "I walked into this room already grateful" attitude. It is gratitude that is indeed radical.

In the words of a modern-day prophet, comedian Stephen Colbert, in an interview with Anderson Cooper in August of 2019:

> It's a gift to exist, and with existence comes suffering. . . . If you are grateful for your life, then you have to be grateful for all of it. You can't pick and choose what you're grateful for. So, what do you get from loss? You get awareness of other people's loss, which allows you to connect with that other person, which allows you to love more deeply and to understand what it's like to be a human being, if it's true that all humans suffer.

To live gratefully is to live as if nothing is promised us. We cultivate an appreciation of the ordinary, marveling at this amazing world of ours, and we experience it as truly

> Gratitude turns what we have into enough.
>
> —Aesop

extraordinary. We can open our eyes to the wonders around us and notice beauty at every turn: the veins in a leaf, the twinkle in the eyes of a child, clear blue skies, the stars at night, a budding tree in the springtime. We draw hot water out of a faucet, have a roof and four walls and machines that automatically wash and dry our clothes. I often think of the refugees in the world who carry water over long distances, cook over an open fire, scrub clothes in a river, and then drape them over rocks, walls, and tree branches to dry. What they would give to have ordinary household amenities like ours! When we begin noticing these everyday gifts, perhaps even writing them down in a gratitude journal, we begin seeing more of them. We're expanding those neural pathways associated with gratefulness and subsequently find more and more opportunities to be grateful. As a friend of mine notes, "I'm just grateful to be on the sunny side of the grass." But we need to practice! All the positive benefits of gratitude cannot be had just by thinking about them. We must put in the time to practice.

Writing about all the good in our lives can make us more aware of these gifts, deepening their emotional impact. Here are some research-based suggestions for maximizing the rewards of keeping a gratitude journal.

Don't just go through the motions. Research suggests that journaling is more effective if you first make the conscious decision to become happier and more grateful.[45]

Perhaps ponder each day as though it is either the first day of your life or the very last day of your life. If you do this, Brother David Steindl-Rast says, you will have spent the day very well. Go for depth over breadth. Elaborating in detail carries more benefits than a superficial list of many things.

Get personal. Focus on *people* to whom you are grateful instead of on things. Try subtraction, not just addition. One effective way of stimulating gratitude is to reflect on what your life would be like *without* certain blessings rather than just tally up all those good things. While cleaning out the garage recently, I found a box filled with letters my husband and I wrote while we lived apart. What would my life be without Jack over the past forty years? That question alone brought a wave of gratitude.

Savor surprises. Record unexpected or surprising events, as these tend to elicit stronger levels of gratitude.

Don't overdo it. We can become numb to the novelty and benefits if we write more frequently. Jotting grateful notes occasionally, once or twice per week, is more beneficial than daily journaling. In fact, one study found that people who wrote in their gratitude journals once a week for six weeks reported boosts in happiness afterward. Those who wrote three times per week didn't receive that boost.[46]

Last spring, my newly painted office was crying out for some semblance of order. A few decades' worth of books sat in piles on the floor, a visual reminder of the many eras in my life. I certainly didn't need every volume in front of me. I took the opportunity to thoughtfully reshelve only what was essential. ("Essential" being used very loosely here.) I pondered each book's future usefulness, retrieving any bookmarks and old letters tucked inside. When I came across a card or letter, I took a few moments to read it and recall the author's gift to my life. These little gems, tucked away long ago, transformed a painful project into a delightful chore. This undertaking became a meditation on the many good souls who have graced my journey, generating within me a sense of deep gratitude.

> Can you see the holiness in those things you take for granted—a paved road or a washing machine? If you concentrate on finding what is good in every situation, you will discover that your life will suddenly be filled with gratitude, a feeling that nurtures the soul.
> —Rabbi Harold Kushner

The power of a handwritten note is immeasurable. I treasure these cards, written in a variety of longhand styles, holding thoughtful sentiments from family, friends, coworkers, mentors, and customers. The books may go, but the letters will stay, reminders of the love that has carried me through the years.

PRACTICE

Ponder all the people who have contributed to who and where you are today. Bring to mind relatives and ancestors who made sacrifices and endured hardships, who perhaps moved to a foreign land. Their courage, strength, and spirit provide you, today, with opportunities you would not have had otherwise. Although we will never meet them in person, we can feel connected to them, experiencing deep appreciation for their lives and vision.

Next, bring into focus all the teachers, mentors, and friends who have impacted your life and taught you how to live and love. Their time, example, and simple presence have influenced us in countless ways. Hold them in your heart, and if some are still with us, consider writing a note of gratitude to them. Be specific and add as much detail as possible, thanking these people for all they have given you. This exercise helps us become more deeply aware of how interconnected we are to one another.

4

LEARNING COMPASSION
AND SERVICE

*I don't know what your destiny will be, but one thing I know:
the only ones among you who will be really happy
are those who have sought and found how to serve.*

—ALBERT SCHWEITZER

In July of 2014, Jose and William arrived in Pittsburgh from Guatemala after a harrowing journey through Mexico atop a train. Just sixteen years old, they hoped to enroll in classes at our suburban high school and needed immunizations and various medical clearances in order to attend. Soon after their arrival, a friend working in the county immigration office asked Jack and me to help them navigate the appointments. "Sure," we said, wholly unaware that saying yes would bring more joy to our lives than we could have imagined.

Early on a Saturday morning in August, I arrived at the home of William, Jose, and Leonel, Jose's older brother. Jose greeted me at the door. After William and Leonel appeared and introduced themselves, we proceeded to my car and drove to the clinic in downtown Pittsburgh. The ride tested my rusty Spanish-speaking skills. Every so often, the three of them would break into Popti, their native tongue.

I smiled at the sound of this foreign language and hoped my facial expressions conveyed my friendliness.

We arrived at the Spanish-speaking facility and joined the line already forming at the doors. For forty-five minutes, everyone waited patiently without a hint of frustration. At eight o'clock the doors opened, and the dual-language nurses and doctors got to work. More waiting ensued, until finally a nurse examined Jose and William. She explained that several rounds of immunizations would be required for them to attend North Allegheny High School. No problem, I said. We would return every few weeks until the boys received all the necessary shots.

During one of our subsequent visits, a dental associate pulled me aside to inform me that Jose and William needed dental work in short order, since they had found serious cavities in both of them. I assured the woman I would find a dentist to help us. The following Monday, I called our friend Dr. Paul, my husband's former physics student. Paul is a thoughtful, kind young man who has been our family dentist for several years. "I'm trying to assist two Guatemalan boys who have serious dental issues but don't have insurance. By any chance are you able to help?" I asked. "Let's take a look," he said. Paul arranged to meet us at his office, and after examining Jose and William, determined that some molars needed to be extracted immediately. Paul recommended his oral surgeon friend, Dr. Wayne, who saw the boys a few days later. After taking X-rays, Dr. Wayne announced that their decayed teeth needed to be taken out as soon as possible, guessing that chewing sugar cane in the fields had gutted them. I explained that they didn't have insurance, and that concern was waved away. "We'll take care of them," Dr. Wayne assured me.

William and Jose were frightened at the prospect of oral surgery. In rural Guatemala, no anesthesia was available, so extreme pain was simply part of tooth removal. I explained, in my very limited Spanish, that they would be put to sleep, they wouldn't feel a thing, and within an hour they'd be awake, eating Popsicles and Jell-o for two days if they wanted.

The surgery was successful, the boys amazed at the easy process and how much better their mouths felt afterwards. They spent part of the weekend at our house recovering, devouring all the soft treats they could consume. When we returned to the clinic a few weeks later for a follow-up visit, the nurse began thanking me for finding dental care for the boys. I explained to her that I was the one who was thankful and felt so fortunate that I knew dentists who could help Jose and William. Dr. Paul and Dr. Wayne were clearly quite happy to be of service, and that was my role: to provide an opportunity for these young men to use their medical skills and improve the lives of Jose and William. What greater joy is there for any of us?

If Christianity has taught me anything, like "love your neighbor as yourself," it has clearly preached that every human being is an expression and image of God. Jose and William's story presents true examples of the corporal and spiritual works of mercy, as practiced for centuries by Catholics and other believers. Every person who offered services, took time to listen, and accompanied these young men expressed the spiritual virtue of charity. We would prefer a world in which the works of mercy were not so critical, but they will always be needed, sometimes desperately. Had the boys been born in the United States, Jose and William would have the world at their feet. But because of the simple fact that their birthplace was rural Guatemala, opportunities for education and employment are virtually nonexistent. After almost six years of countless legal appointments and hurdles, Jose now has a visa, a Social Security card, and a path to citizenship. He has also become like an adopted son. (William, meanwhile, continues to be mentored by a Pittsburgh Sister of Charity.) He's working toward his high school equivalency exam, learning to drive, and hopes to attend college one day. He dreams of starting a business, perhaps bringing work to his village in Guatemala.

We have learned so much and experienced true happiness through mentoring Jose. We also more keenly appreciate the very basics of life: education, paved roads,

> "I was a stranger and you welcomed me."
> —Matthew 25:35

access to medical care, healthy food choices. His gratitude knows no bounds as he takes advantage of the new opportunities in his adopted homeland. It is with deep joy that we watch Jose learn and grow and become a valuable member of our Pittsburgh community.

PRACTICE

Many communities in the United States have immigrant-outreach centers. Even an hour or two of your time can make a difference in the lives of immigrants: driving them to a legal appointment, accompanying them to a doctor's visit, or assisting with a bank transaction. Knowing a bit of Spanish (or another language) helps but often is not necessary.

The word *compassion* comes from Latin, meaning "to suffer with" or "to suffer together." It's the feeling that arises when we witness another's suffering and we're prompted to relieve that suffering. Current

> The most satisfying thing in life is to have been able to give a large part of one's self to others.
> —Pierre Teilhard de Chardin

research on compassion lists five of its key elements:

- We recognize suffering and notice the impact of events on another person: their anguish or agony.
- We understand the universality of human suffering, that none of us is exempt from the reality that life is sometimes difficult.

- We feel for the person suffering, such as a friend who has shared a loss or sad news.
- We tolerate uncomfortable feelings. We notice what it's like to hold those feelings, perhaps softening our heart toward the person suffering.
- We may be motivated to act to alleviate suffering.[47]

Compassion is not pity but is sympathetic concern for another. It does not imply agreement with the person. We can feel compassion for those whose views are much different from our own, or for those who have mistreated us, while not necessarily condoning their behavior. Compassion helps us get along in community and take care of offspring. "Compassion asks us to go where it hurts, to enter into places of pain, to share in brokenness, fear, confusion, and anguish. . . . Compassion means full immersion in the condition of being human."[48] Most of the world's religious traditions, including Christianity, place compassion at the center of their belief systems.

> If we say, oh, the practice of compassion is something holy, nobody will listen. If we say, warm-heartedness really reduces your blood pressure, your anxiety, your stress and improves your health, then people pay attention.
>
> —The Dalai Lama

Dr. James Doty journeyed from an impoverished childhood to become a renowned neurosurgeon at Stanford. He helped found the Center for Compassion and Altruism Research and Education (CCARE) at Stanford University, which explores the connection between neuroscience, psychology, and contemplative traditions. Those who work at CCARE seek to understand the relationships linking the mind and the heart. Doty calls the work they do the "Science of Compassion."

One of the center's findings is that a life focused on service and outreach often brings a longer, happier life, an outcome not surprising to most of us. Many studies show that when we serve others in a meaningful way, like the dentists Drs. Paul and Wayne, we will likely have stronger immune systems and experience lower inflammation in our cells. Because inflammation invites health concerns such as cancer, heart disease, diabetes, Alzheimer's disease, and even depression, we want to keep it at bay.[49]

Additionally, having strong connections with others, which we create through service, helps us stave off loneliness and recover more quickly from disease and stressful situations. Our bodies are healthier when we care for others, and we'll have fewer aches and pains. One study showed that those who volunteered for at least two hundred hours per year were forty percent less likely to have high blood pressure four years later than those who did not volunteer.[50]

We will also have a greater sense of purpose and meaning. But here's the catch: we receive these benefits only when we serve for the sake of serving, when our motivation is altruistic. If we help others only to get the health advantages, the benefits will escape us. We must serve *authentically*. We may think the world is governed by the survival of the fittest, but it's more accurate to say that we are sustained through "survival of the kindest." Humans are hardwired to support one another and care for others, helping and cooperating with members of our communities. And we aren't alone: other animals, including rats and monkeys, also care for the suffering members of their species.

Serving others also helps build cognitive reserve, which is the brain's ability to maintain normal functioning despite neural declines. With cognitive reserve, we are able to improvise and find alternate ways of solving a problem. Remember, the brain can change the way it operates throughout our life span. Our habits and routines—everything we do and everything we don't do—can either boost our cognitive abilities or weaken them. Building cognitive reserve creates new neural connections, helping us cope with mental challenges as we grow older. By offering compassion to our sisters and brothers, we support the health of our bodies, brains, and souls.[51]

PRACTICE

Choose just one day this week, when you are out and about, to bring an extra dose of compassionate awareness to others. For example, in the grocery checkout line, let a person go in front of you who seems to be in a hurry or who has just a few items in her hands. Let another shopper have the parking spot closer to the entrance. Make eye contact with each clerk you encounter, and thank them by name. It might be the only time a customer calls them by name all day. And we never know how much that person will appreciate it.

When we share the goodness in our own hearts, we unlock the goodness in others.

A person whose life and actions have deeply inspired me is Mister Rogers. He lived in Pittsburgh, my adopted hometown, and I heard many stories about him before he died. Although I discovered him as an adult, he impressed me with his gentle, caring manner, extended to every person he met. The characteristic most often cited by

> A good deed doesn't just evaporate and disappear. Its consequences saturate the universe and the goodness that happens somewhere, anywhere, helps in the transfiguration of the ugliness.
>
> —Bishop Desmond Tutu

those who encountered him was that they felt as if they were the most important person in the world in those moments of interaction with him. He was fully present to them in a way that was astonishing. Fred Rogers looked for the best in everyone and believed that in loving and appreciating our neighbor, we participate in something sacred. I wholeheartedly agree.

Although his main form of service was through his children's television show, Mister Rogers was also known to write letters almost daily to folks who served others: crossing guards, janitors, teachers, nurses, and so on. In 1998, I retrieved a letter from my post office box with a trolley car on the return address, opened the envelope, and found a handwritten letter on trolley stationery from Fred Rogers, thanking me for the messages on my greeting cards. As you can imagine, I was stunned and honored that Mister Rogers was using my cards to convey his thoughts to others. That letter is now framed and hangs in the Cards by Anne packaging room for all to see, reminding us that our work serves those who send and receive our cards.

> Imagine what our real neighborhoods would be like if each of us offered, as a matter of course, just one kind word to another person.
>
> —Fred Rogers

When our lives become packed with responsibilities, appointments, and obligations, it's easy to forget that one of the best gifts we can give others is the simple act of caring. That is the essence of Mister Rogers's example. Take the time to care for one another. Do you know that a lack of time is one of the most common barriers to practicing compassion? When we feel rushed and sense that our time is being squeezed, our willingness to stop and help others is drastically decreased.

Finally, when we teach children the joys of serving and giving, it's important that we not offer rewards for their kind actions. That has been found to decrease motivation. Children can discover the down-deep satisfaction that comes from helping others, hopefully launching them onto a path of lifelong service and compassion.

> The fruit of love is service, which is compassion in action.
>
> —St. Teresa of Calcutta

Several religious traditions teach the importance of cultivating a meditation practice, mainly because these practices cultivate a deep, abiding compassion for others. The "goal" of contemplative prayer is not to just feel peaceful and calm, although that can be one of its benefits. A meditation practice should send us back into the arms of the world, in the words of Thomas Merton, so we can continue our work with greater compassion and understanding toward those we serve. Chuck Raison at Emory University has shown that a regular compassion meditation practice reduces negative responses to stress, including physical, psychological, and behavioral responses.[52] In other words, nurturing quiet prayer time and holding others' intentions winds up benefiting our health and well-being. Remarkable, I think!

Sr. Simone Campbell is a member of the Sisters of Social Service, and she aims to live up to her community's name. She knows the importance of listening and responding to the needs of those around us. But Sr. Simone observes that we often expect ourselves to fix everything and then become overwhelmed. "That is not our job!" she insists. We should try to do just one thing, because if we think we must take care of every problem, we become paralyzed and do nothing. She advises us to listen deeply to the stories of others, see where they lead, then simply do our part. You don't have to do it all. She said, "Being in community means doing my part, no more, no less."

This advice has been quite helpful to me. It can be overwhelming when we come face-to-face with the vast needs of others in our community. Recently I accompanied Jose to a GED orientation meeting. At one point, the director of the program asked the twenty-three attendees to verbalize their goals. One young man raised his hand and said, "I just want to survive." Several others nodded in agreement. Later, when the director mentioned that the cost to take the GED course was $120, many of the attendees uttered a hopeless sigh. She quickly reassured them that scholarships would be available. Sitting around the large table with these adults gave me insight into the enormous challenges some of them face every day. I want to help every person in that room but know that I don't have the time or resources to do so.

Remembering Sr. Simone's words, "Do your part. No more. No less." keeps me from despair.

Several years ago, our daughter Sarah found a way to do her part. At the time, she had two daughters under the age of three—her life was already full. Then she discovered Eats on Feets, a Facebook community for young mothers that matches women with extra breast milk with those who are unable to nurse. (Sounds like communities of old, yes?) Sarah was producing double what her baby girl needed, so she found two women who were looking for milk. One of the babies was born with a chromosomal disorder and could tolerate human milk much better than formula. The families were thrilled to get nearly fifteen hundred ounces of milk between them, and Sarah was happy to provide sustenance to these growing babies. So, even with long, busy "mom" days, she did her part.

As Dr. Martin Luther King, Jr. put it: "Everybody can be great. Because everybody can serve. You don't have to have a college degree to serve. You don't have to make your subject and your verb agree to serve. You only need a heart full of grace." Every person can participate. Regardless of station or situation, you can find creative ways to give of yourself.

My friend Dan owns a large hair salon in Pittsburgh. Although only in his thirties, Dan has built a very successful business while also becoming one of our city's most prolific fundraisers. The mission of his salon is "Make it a better world," and boy does he live that motto! In fact, if you didn't know better, you might think he was running a nonprofit organization. Most months, Dan advertises a charity opportunity for an organization: breast cancer research, the Cystic Fibrosis Foundation, organ donation registration, or blood collection. Last Christmas, for example, his salon collected more than eight hundred new blankets, which he distributed on Christmas Eve. He spent that day passing out blankets to residents in the tent city where the homeless sleep, and to patients in children's hospitals and veterans' hospitals. Dan said that if someone had offered him a Mercedes that day in exchange for his experience, he would have turned them down in a flash.

Why would a young man forgo holiday celebrations to pass out blankets to strangers? Because Dan finds enormous satisfaction in helping others, bringing light and love to so many who would otherwise be neglected. On another Christmas Eve, he brought small gifts to hospital patients who would be spending the holiday alone.

> [W]e have the power to create joy and happiness by our simplest acts of caring and compassion. . . . [W]e have the power to unlock the goodness in other people's hearts by sharing the goodness in ours.
>
> —Kent Nerburn

He noted that it's not really the gift that is most appreciated but the time he spends with each person. Sometimes he concludes a visit by singing "Silent Night" or another carol in his beautiful tenor voice. He often leaves patients in tears, their hearts filled with joy and gratitude. Dan lives his belief that all of us can make a difference by caring for one another, one person at a time. And in that caring, we will bring happiness to ourselves and others.

PRACTICE

Is there someone you serve in your job, or work with, or know in your neighborhood, who needs a listening ear or a friendly visit? Perhaps it is someone you have previously overlooked or judged for one reason or another. Take a few minutes and reach out to them. With the growing epidemic of loneliness in our country, you will be doing your part to thwart this broadening problem.

Remember that being compassionate increases oxytocin levels and lowers inflammation, anxiety, and stress. Oxytocin also makes us feel more loving, trusting, and secure. Showing kindness to another activates the reward circuitry in our brains. So we will not only be *doing* good, we will also *feel* good.

We might not think of our daily commute as an opportunity for compassion, but it certainly can be. The practice can also bring a sense of calm and presence to our day. Whether we drive in traffic or take public transportation, the experience can be stressful for various reasons. We may be faced with unexpected delays, rude drivers, or annoying passengers. But there are ways to bring a sense of compassion to that part of our day.

Some of the following suggestions were inspired by *Mindful* magazine's tips:[53]

1. **Use stop signs, traffic lights, or commuter stops to build "presence" muscles.** When you come to a full stop, inhale deeply and bring awareness to this moment. You might add a simple prayer of thanksgiving. When you continue moving again, take care to notice the sights and sounds. Our senses provide glimpses into the gifts all around us and keep our thoughts anchored in the present moment. It's so easy for our minds to jump to worry about the day ahead or regrets about yesterday. When we resist this mind-wandering, we strengthen our attention skills.

2. **Practice yielding to increase your awareness of compassion.** We tend to press and maneuver to get where we're going as quickly as possible, often with irritation lurking just below the surface. This pits us against other commuters in a frantic competition, which certainly doesn't engender compassion. Our internal dialogue may sound like this: *Can't that driver pay attention when the light turns green?* or *Why isn't that person ahead of me walking faster, or letting me pass?* Instead of welcoming frustration, we can try yielding to others as a spiritual practice. We might reach our destination a few minutes later, but this open-hearted, gentle attitude might transform our commute time for

the better. We could even offer a prayer for others: "May he be safe. May she be happy." Ponder how their lives might have more difficulty than yours, and yield to them. Your stress will lower, and your health will benefit.

3. **Notice yourself rushing.** When I hit several red lights in a row, my first instinct is to feel irritation. When I get in a waiting line that is moving much slower than the others, I grow frustrated. By noticing these feelings and bodily sensations, I can remind myself to be calm and patient. When I remember to practice this, I become more aware of others and can bring more compassion and kindness to my interactions with them. That's much healthier than the agitation I might generate through rushing.

All of this takes practice and determination. Just choose one of these suggestions to integrate into your commute. You'll experience more calm and generate more compassion toward everyone on your journey. As Henry David Thoreau said, "Nothing can be more useful . . . than a determination not to be hurried."

From the last half of Danusha Laméris's poem "Small Kindnesses"

> We want to be handed our cup of coffee hot,
> and to say thank you to the person handing it. To smile
> at them and for them to smile back. For the waitress
> to call us honey when she sets down the bowl of clam
>   chowder,
> and for the driver in the red pick-up truck to let us pass.
> We have so little of each other, now. So far
> from tribe and fire. Only these brief moments of exchange.
> What if they are the true dwelling of the holy, these
> fleeting temples we make together when we say, "Here, have
>   my seat," "Go ahead—you first," "I like your hat."[54]

When she was just seven years old, my niece Sadie became a shelter buddy. The St. Louis Humane Society put out a call for child volunteers to help calm dogs, and Sadie raised her hand. Research shows that when children read to frightened and stressed-out animals, the animals respond positively and are more adoptable. Sadie loves animals and needed to practice her new reading skills, so it was a perfect match for a summer activity. She would read to a few four-legged friends and help soothe their anxiety and discomfort.

> Judge tenderly, if you must. There is usually a side you have not heard, a story you know nothing about, and a battle waged that you are not having to fight.
> —Traci Lea LaRussa

At the start of her first day, Sadie found a very agitated dog barking incessantly. She sat on the floor next to his cage, book in hand, and began reading. At first, he continued to bark, and one of the employees asked if she'd like to try working with another dog. She said, "No, I'll keep going," and continued for a while. Sure enough, after a few more pages, the dog stopped barking and sat down in front of Sadie to listen. A mother and toddler walked by, looking for a dog, and stopped to watch the reading session. When the story was finished, Sadie left the room to tour the facility, and upon returning, discovered that the mom had decided to adopt the dog. She was thrilled, experiencing what the Ecclesiastes author meant by being happy and doing good.

> I know that there is nothing better for them than to be happy and enjoy themselves as long as they live.
> —Ecclesiastes 3:12

Our world is filled with suffering, and if we can make things a little better for those around us, we live happier, longer lives. Each of us can do something, as Sadie discovered. All of us, young and old, have some gift to share, some good to bring to the world. What is yours?

PRACTICE

What are your talents and interests? What "sparks joy" in you? Take some time to think about those questions, and then reach out to a local agency that needs someone like you. Just commit to volunteering for an hour or two and see if it's a good match. Your local nursing homes need story readers and song leaders. Head to the soup kitchen if you enjoy cooking. If you like books and reading, volunteer at your local library. If gardening is your thing, plant flowers with your community's garden organization. If you enjoy nature trails, join a group that restores and cleans local paths. These are just a few of the possibilities to share your interests and make the world a better place. You will become happier and healthier as a result.

Bishop Desmond Tutu reminds us that "We are each made for goodness, love and compassion. Our lives are transformed as much as the world is when we live with these truths."

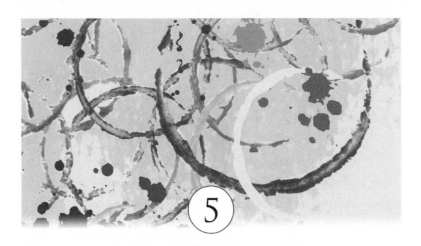

NURTURING COMMUNITY AND RELATIONSHIPS

Sometimes our light goes out,
but is blown again into instant flame
by an encounter with another
human being.
Each of us owes the deepest thanks
to those who have rekindled this
inner light.

—ALBERT SCHWEITZER

On a summer weekend, Jack and I tackled some long-overdue home projects, necessitating numerous trips to our local hardware store. At the outset, I decided to make a conscious effort to address each store helper by name instead of concentrating on efficiency and speed. This subtle change affected the quality of my conversations more than anticipated. As Jesse loaded bags of mulch into my car, he recounted his struggles in school due to a few learning disabilities and how he was hoping to join the Marines in the next few years. Stan cut and recut pipes several times, a consequence of my inexperience in the "DIY curtain rod" department. As I exited the store for the fifth time, Stan called out, "I guess I'll see you again tonight!" I laughed and replied, "I hope not!" The simple practice of acknowledging each store associate transformed these brief interactions into genuine personal encounters.

We sometimes forget that simple concept: those we encounter throughout our daily lives are people, with families and friends, and dreams and burdens alike. They each have a story to tell, containing joy and heartbreak, just like you and me. This week, as we start each day, let's set an intention to be present to each person we encounter. If you meet any "helpers," address them by name. This easy act will immediately announce that you recognize their personhood, not just their worker role. You might keep in mind, too, that those who are serving us may be struggling with unspoken challenges. Scottish author Ian MacLaren reminds us to "be kind, one to another, for most of us are fighting a hard battle."

Bring a little more presence, a little more attention, to everyone you meet. Who knows, your kindnesses might rekindle the inner light of those you encounter.

PRACTICE

A friend creates table tent cards a few inches wide, with affirmations for waitstaff, cashiers, and store clerks. She writes uplifting phrases on them such as "Thank you!" "You're Awesome!" "Glad Our Paths Crossed." "Keep Shining!" and tucks them into her wallet. When she's out and about, she leaves a card with cashiers or clerks or with her tip at restaurants. It's a small way of sending kindness and love to the people she meets.

Create a few table tents for yourself. Find scraps of sturdy paper and a marker. Cut the paper into three-by-three-inch squares or smaller, and fold them in half. Decorate with an affirmation and a sticker or hand-drawn flower, leaf, or star. You'll spread cheer wherever you leave them!

In the Christian tradition, one of the most powerful passages about community is found in 1 Corinthians 12:14, 21–26:

> Now the body is not a single part, but many. . . . The eye cannot say to the hand, "I do not need you," nor again the head to the feet, "I do not need you." Indeed, the parts of the body that seem to be weaker are all the more necessary, and those parts of the body that we consider less honorable we surround with greater honor, and our less presentable parts are treated with greater propriety, whereas our more presentable parts do not need this. But God has so constructed the body as to give greater honor to a part that is without it, so that there may be no division in the body, but that the parts may have the same concern for one another. If [one] part suffers, all the parts suffer with it; if one part is honored, all the parts share its joy.

What a simple yet profound way to see ourselves in relation with others! No one goes through this life alone. And whatever happens to anyone has an impact on the rest of us. We feel it in our bones when a community member suffers a great loss. It is true: "If one part suffers, all the parts suffer with it." We have experienced this as our country and world strains under the losses caused by the coronavirus. Saint Paul's insightful metaphor inspires us to live, individually and collectively, with mercy, kindness, justice, and peace.

> We never know how our small activities will affect others through the invisible fabric of our connectedness.
> —Grace Lee Boggs

PRACTICE

Where can we show mercy, kindness, or compassion? Churches and other organizations offer unlimited opportunities for community building and service projects. There are many in need of helping hands or legs or voices. Volunteer in an area that interests you, perhaps one in which you have special skills. Do you enjoy sending cards of encouragement? Offer to join the bereavement support group and write notes to shut-ins. Do you have musical skills? Join the choir or entertain nursing home residents near you. These are just two examples of how you can help sustain and honor other parts of the body and "share in its joy."

It's not surprising to learn that, from a scientific viewpoint as well, our close relationships keep us healthy: good friends are like night watchmen. How can that be? Our friends' presence in daily life protects our telomeres because they help us handle the blows and challenges that come along. Social contact protects our cognitive function as we age, and our cells send out fewer pro-inflammatory signals, decreasing our risk of heart disease and stroke more than obesity and hypertension. Research also indicates that happily married people have longer telomeres and a lower risk of early mortality. Loneliness and social isolation actually affect our health as much as light smoking would.[55]

I know that there is nothing better for them than to be happy and enjoy themselves as long as they live.

—Ecclesiastes 3:12

We find that "weak ties" are also important, as they buffer against stress and loneliness, boosting our physical and psychological health. So-called weak ties are acquaintances we see occasionally and people we see for a specific purpose. My weak ties include pharmacy interns, clerks at the FedEx store, and Joe, who delivers our cards and envelopes. They aren't close friends, but I know their names, and we chat a bit when we see each other. Maintaining various social roles is associated with better cognitive functioning, better emotional and physical health, and decreased risk of mortality in later life. Psychologists know that people with high levels of social integration—those in a broad range of relationships, both intimate and casual—tend to be healthier and happier.

I recently had a lovely exchange with a "weak tie" in my world. On a visit to Trader Joe's, Chris, a new associate, informed me that their beloved manager Amie had accepted a post at a TJ's in Indianapolis. She was a founding mother of our five-year-old store, and Chris said her last day would be Thursday. "I must bring a card to wish her well," I told Chris.

A few minutes later, as I was checking out, Chris brought a small bouquet of flowers to the cashier. "These are for you, Anne." I smiled and thanked him and vowed to follow through on my intention. (One good deed deserves another, right?) On Thursday morning, I selected a card and tucked the matching bookmark and magnet inside. The message read, "And suddenly you know: It's time to start something new and trust the magic of beginnings." I jotted a quick note to Amie, thanking her for creating a store with a wonderful, friendly atmosphere. I wrote her name in calligraphy on the envelope and headed to TJ's. I found Amie checking out customers and stood in her line, watching her greet a new customer with her wide smile and usual friendliness. When it was my turn, I handed her the envelope, saying, "I heard today is your last day here and just wanted to thank you for all you've done to make this a great place to shop." Her eyes welled up with tears as she gave me a big hug, saying, "You have no idea how much that means to me. No idea." I wished her good luck in her adventure. Of course, I was now crying, too, touched by how much this small gesture meant to her.

I drove home with joy in my heart, reminding me how "our small activities will affect others." So, keep conversing with those you know, and nurture a new "weak tie" or two in your corner of the world.

PRACTICE: HONE YOUR LISTENING SKILLS

This week, when you're in a conversation, listen intently to the other person. Notice their tone of voice, inflection, and body language while they are talking. Observe your internal reactions and your body language while you listen. Try not to jump ahead and formulate your response. Listen and let the person finish their thought before rushing in to respond. Simply attend to what the person is saying, both with their words and with their body language. Try to increase the amount of listening you do each day, gradually speaking less and listening more. You will probably feel happier, honoring the other person and living more fully in the present moment.

Connectedness is usually a great blessing. We rejoice in the ability to communicate with family members across the globe and even see their faces while we talk. Our seven-year-old granddaughter regularly chats via FaceTime with my mom and dad, who are eighty-eight and ninety years old.

> I like flaws and feel more comfortable around people who have them. I myself am made entirely of flaws, stitched together with good intentions.
> —Augusten Burroughs

We laugh and joke with our other grandchildren regularly and keep up to date on all their milestones and school events. What a gift it is to all of us!

But our hyperconnected world also brings images of suffering and loss to us on a daily basis, and it is difficult to take it all in. Pictures and videos of devastation from natural and human-made disasters are heartbreaking. We can send donations to agencies and offer prayers for those affected and the helpers providing services, but it can be overwhelming.

When our thinking and emotions are driven by external events such as these, we can become anxious and upset. Psychological research reminds us that self-awareness

> We are like islands in the sea, separate on the surface but connected in the deep.
> —William James

and mindfulness help us cope better. With our thoughts rooted in the present moment, we remain conscious of our emotions and our thoughts instead of sinking into despair. This awareness allows us to handle stress more productively, whether it's the result of a difficult situation in our own life or in a far-off stranger's life. Staying grounded in the present, we recall the gifts we do have and can offer, whether large or small. We can be grateful for the fabric of our connectedness and our ability to contribute our unique threads to that fabric.

The communication networks of forest trees highlight the fact that humanity is not the only species that relies on its members for survival. Research from Canadian forest ecologist Suzanne Simard, among others, reveals that trees of the same species are communal, forming alliances with trees of other species, as well. Scientists would argue that trees don't possess human traits, but they also aren't disconnected loners competing for water, sunlight, and nutrients. Although not conscious, trees have evolved to biologically cooperate in order to remain alive, similar to insect colonies. Forest trees communicate through underground fungal networks, like pipelines, that connect their root systems. Nutrients, carbon, and water are exchanged between the trees as needed. For example, when several trees are under insect attack or struggling to survive, they send out chemicals indicating distress, which other trees pick up. The healthy trees, through these fungal networks, send more nutrients to the needy trees, saving the weaker ones. When the oldest trees in a forest are felled, the survival rate of younger trees is substantially diminished, because older trees have a greater number of roots and established networks.

This research does not imply that trees have human qualities, but it illustrates that all communities and ecosystems benefit from cooperation and interconnectedness.

> My humanity is bound up with yours, for we can only be human together.
> —Bishop Desmond Tutu

Trees live longer in healthy, stable, collaborative forests. Similarly, when every member of our human society is acknowledged and valued, when we pull together and share resources, the whole community is stronger. I'm inspired by these tree networks, knowing that human and nonhuman worlds thrive when we care for the vulnerable in our presence. Who knew that forests hold these lessons about how to cooperate and maintain our communities' health?

The next time you walk in a forest, think about the vast networks working to sustain life just below your feet. How can we not be awed by nature's intricacies?

PRACTICE

Are there any friends or relatives with whom you've lost touch? Perhaps send them a note to schedule a visit or phone call and rekindle your relationship. Is there something you love to do but have been putting off until it's the "right" time? Perhaps you could begin putting a plan into motion. Can you express your feelings to someone who might appreciate knowing how you feel? And finally, are you living the life you imagined for yourself? Are you opening the door to happiness in your life? It's never too late to take a step across that threshold. Remember, Grandma Moses began painting at the ripe age of seventy-eight.

After a recent Labor Day weekend, I returned to my desk awash in deep joy after witnessing the wedding of Melissa, our daughter's lifelong friend. As she married Jon, we observed up close the beauty of love and human relationships. The groom

> To love at all is to be vulnerable. Love anything, and your heart will certainly be wrung and possibly be broken.
> —C. S. Lewis

choked back tears as the bride walked down the aisle. The father of the bride struggled to keep his composure as he shook the groom's hand and led his daughter to the steps of the altar. The bride's hands and voice trembled as she recited her vows, reflecting wholehearted love. I carried these joyful moments with me as my workday began.

The first task that Tuesday was to speak with John, an older gentleman who needed sympathy cards and thank-you notes. He also inquired about our Christmas cards. John's account and last name were up on our computer screen, but with a woman's first name. I told him he could go online and see our entire collection, and with that remark, he began to cry. "Oh, John, I'm so sorry. Was Ann your wife?" He took a while to collect himself, and choking back tears, said, "Yes. We were married for fifty-two years, and she just died. She and I would look at cards together on your website."

The designs he ordered would be used as acknowledgments for those who attended her funeral. I asked him about her last days, if he had family and friends nearby, and I expressed sympathy for his loss. My eyes were filled with tears from experiencing this gentleman's profound sorrow and deep love for his wife, and I hung up the phone with a heavy heart

> All of our regrets come from a lack of courage.
> —Bronnie Ware

It struck me how, in the span of thirty-six hours, I had observed both the overflowing joy and overwhelming sorrow that come from loving another. And that to love is to be vulnerable. Great beauty is found in that vulnerability. So I will try to heed the advice attributed to St. Benedict: "Always we begin again!" Begin again and rededicate myself to express the gratitude and tenderness I feel for those I love.

> Ours is not the task of fixing the entire world all at once, but of stretching out to mend the part of the world that is within our reach.
> —Clarissa Pinkola Estés

With the ephemeral nature of life in mind, an article titled "The Art of Condolence" caught my attention. It notes how important it is to express sympathy to someone who is grieving the loss of a loved one. Here are a few of its wise words of advice:

1. **Being tongue-tied is OK.** Admitting you're at a loss for words is better and more caring than offering a trite saying like "At least he died doing something he loved." or "They're in a better place." Just say, "I'm so sorry. I don't know what to say."

2. **Share a positive memory.** Those are always appreciated, and the family may not have heard your story of their loved one.

3. **Do something.** Facebook and other social media expressions are not enough. They are a start, but you must send a letter of condolence to the friend or family member. They will certainly appreciate a handwritten note from you, especially if it contains a memory about their loved one. Baked goods, gift cards, flowers, and offers to walk the dog are also greatly appreciated. Knowing that others are thinking of you is very comforting. As John, who lost his wife, Ann, wrote to me, "I never get tired of hearing that friends and family, even people I don't know, are praying for me. It means *so much*."

4. **There is no time limit on sympathy.** Certainly people appreciate the cards and letters sent immediately after their loss. But sometimes sending a note a month or two afterward is especially valued, when everyone returns to their lives and reality of the loss sets in. Notes arriving on the deceased person's birthday, a couple's anniversary, or other meaningful occasions are also treasured.

We rely on our friends to forgive us. None of us is perfect, and we count on our long-time friends to tolerate our mistakes and love us despite our shortcomings, and we

> Friendship isn't a big thing.
> It's a million little things.
> —Unknown

do the same for them. We accompany one another on this journey, witnessing one another's lives, "walking each other home," as a popular quote observes. It is a great gift to know some friends for decades, people who have believed in us, supported us, listened to us, comforted us. Our journeys are so much more meaningful, more bearable, more joyful, when we walk with others who care for us, when they truly see us and we see them. No masks, no armor, no costumes hiding our real selves. We connect on a deep level, and that is something to celebrate. Thank goodness for our friends' generosity of spirit.

Thanks, too, for our friends' abilities to make us laugh and smile. Science and spiritual teachers would agree that the smiles on our faces can transform us and everyone around us. Neuroscience research shows that the act of smiling is good for our brains, our bodies, and those we meet throughout the day. When we smile, our brains generate feel-good chemicals such as dopamine, endorphins, and serotonin, all of which conspire to make us feel happy. These neurotransmitters reduce stress, which can lower our blood pressure and heart rates while boosting our immune systems. In addition, endorphins are natural pain relievers, and serotonin serves as an antidepressant.

Smiling is contagious because of the part of our brains called the cingulate cortex, an unconscious automatic response area responsible for facial expression. We can't help but mimic another person who's smiling; it actually takes a conscious effort on our part to suppress a smile. (Try it sometime.) I smile, you smile, she smiles, he smiles: it's a classic ripple effect.

So go ahead and spread some sunshine into every room you enter today. You will feel happier while simultaneously boosting your immune system and heart function. You'll also bring cheer, maybe even better health, into the lives of your friends, family, and coworkers.[56]

Want a reason to postpone cosmetic surgery or a Botox injection? Researchers find that people whose facial expressions are hindered, as they are with procedures such as these, are less able to interpret other people's facial expressions. We use our faces to manage our social interactions, and the less nuance we perceive, the more difficult it is to recognize emotions and nurture relationships. Facial muscle movement is important if we want to continue recognizing and internalizing the emotions of those around us.[57]

Melissa is a classmate of mine who looks for ways to promote better communication and deeper relationships within her young family. As part of an assignment, she wrote the following three questions for her family to discuss at the dinner table:

1. What made you laugh today?
2. What made you proud today?
3. What did you see that was beautiful today?

The questions capture lightheartedness, self-awareness, mindfulness, attentiveness, and gratitude. So many lessons in one simple exercise fostering real sharing and connection. If you have a young family, you might want to pull out your phone and record some of these answers. My adult children love watching old videos of themselves answering serious questions. Just think of the many opportunities you may have, decades from now, to savor these moments again.

6

DEVELOPING EMPATHY AND KINDNESS

Empathy is "changing places . . . with the sufferer."
—ADAM SMITH

The German word for *empathy* is *Einfuhlung*, which literally means "feeling into." Empathy is the ability to understand another person's feelings and perceptions and using that understanding to guide our actions. It's a human characteristic, of course, but it is also observed in our primate cousins. Frans de Wall, a famous primatologist, posits that empathy is both an inborn trait and a learned skill. He and other scientists have documented hundreds of displays of consolation and empathy in their subjects. For example, they've witnessed a young chimpanzee embracing a screaming adult male after the latter was defeated in a fight. They've also watched monkeys refusing to pull a chain for food when it simultaneously delivered a shock to a companion. One primate in this experiment wouldn't eat for twelve days, basically starving itself, because of its reluctance to harm the other animal.[58]

This capacity for empathy probably evolved in humans because it helped our ancestors survive. The reasons for this are twofold: one, good parents respond to their children's needs. Of course, they show love and empathy to their offspring, who they hope will grow and thrive. Two, our species can be sustained only if we cooperate with one another. If I help you when you are in need, you'll take care of me when I'm in need. This empathic reciprocity helps us all survive, because living in a cooperative community ensures the safety and well-being of all of its members.

But empathy is fragile. Among our close animal relatives, it is switched on by events within their grouping, such as a youngster in distress. But it is just as easily switched off with regard to outsiders or members of other species, such as prey. Our evolutionary background makes it hard to identify with outsiders. We've evolved to ignore people we barely know and to distrust folks who don't look like us. Even if we are largely cooperative within our communities, we can become a different animal in our treatment of strangers. It is important to be aware of this innate tendency to separate "us" from "them."

The familiar but timeless Good Samaritan parable illustrates this point perfectly: our neighbor is *anyone* we meet. If we encounter a person in need, we are called to

> "Love one another as I have loved you."
> —John 15:12

show empathy and compassion, even to those not in our social circles. There is no "them." If we call ourselves Christian, we care for our sisters and brothers everywhere.

As a traditional Gaelic Rune of Hospitality reminds us:

> Often, often, often
> Goes the Christ in the stranger's guise.
> Often, often, often
> Goes the Christ in the stranger's guise.

PRACTICE

This week, seek an opportunity to talk with someone whose life may be very different from yours: the neighbor from another country or ethnic group, a store clerk, an acquaintance who is much younger or older than you. It doesn't have to be a long conversation. You can begin by calling them by their name, looking them clearly in the eyes, and asking a simple question, such as "Cathy, do you work here full-time?" or "Andre, how is your day going so far?" Using their name means you are acknowledging each one as a person, not just as the role or job they're doing. Open your ears and listen and try to find similarities in your lives. We are more alike than we are different.

A few years ago, while working at my exhibit booth in Anaheim, California, I welcomed a customer and helped her find a few items. Although only fortysomething, Karen was scooting around in a motorized chair. After chatting for a while, I asked what condition caused her to need that assistance. She explained she'd had surgery a few years ago to correct a foot issue, but the operation was unsuccessful and worsened the problem. Now she is no longer able to walk. Karen shared her struggles and disappointments without self-pity, but her pain was clear. She hopes for gradual improvement, but the road ahead isn't easy, and it's uncertain if she'll ever walk again. I was inspired by her courage and fortitude in the face of such challenges.

> Could a greater miracle take place than for us to look through each other's eyes for an instant?
> —Henry David Thoreau

The next day, I spied Karen waiting patiently at the edge of our booth. After finishing up with another customer, I greeted her. She smiled broadly and said, "I needed to come back and tell you how much our conversation about my disability meant to me. It's so helpful to talk about these issues, but most folks avoid the subject. Thank you for caring and listening."

Karen's words reminded me that every person wants to be seen and heard. One definition of empathy is the ability to be wholly present with someone. It's not what we say, and certainly not what we think. It's the ability to simply *be* with another, with an open heart, nonjudgmentally. We aren't

> Empathy is really important. Only when our clever brain and our human heart work together in harmony can we achieve our true potential.
> —Jane Goodall

perfect, and we're going to mess it up sometimes. But it doesn't take extraordinary talent or effort or insight. Just being an interested human being, witnessing another's pain or joy, is all that's required. Where there is empathy, we find more joy, happiness, and closer social connections.

Empathy comes in two distinct forms: *cognitive empathy* and *affective empathy*. Cognitive empathy functions when we take the perspective of the other person and put

> For dialogue to take place, there has to be . . . empathy.
> —Pope Francis

ourselves in the other's place. Children exhibit this in their first few years, indicating that humans are wired for empathy. As I listened to Karen talk about not being able to walk, it was easy to imagine how difficult it would be if I were confined to a wheelchair. I experienced cognitive empathy. Affective empathy means we share or mirror the other person's emotions, including both positive and negative emotions. It might be described as "your pain in my heart." So, as I chatted with Karen, the heaviness I felt would indicate this affective empathy. We build emotional connections with others when we observe someone struggling and feel their pain within us.

The discovery of mirror neurons in 1992 was heralded as a breakthrough in empathy research. What are mirror neurons? They are brain cells that react both when a particular action is performed and when it is simply observed. Italian researchers found that monkeys' mirror neurons fired in response to witnessing another's emotion, such as pain, in the same way as if the monkeys were themselves in pain. These scientists believe this discovery proves we are hardwired for empathy, helping explain how humans "read" other people's hearts and feel empathy for them. However, other scientists are not certain the results can be transferred so seamlessly to humans. Cambridge psychologist Simon Baron-Cohen believes we need to be careful about equating mirror neurons' existence with empathy in human beings. He and other researchers posit that mirror neurons are a small part of an empathy circuit that encompasses at least ten interconnected brain regions.[59] Whichever viewpoint is most accurate, these mirror neurons seem to play some role in our ability to "feel into" others and connect with them. Continuing research will certainly shed more light on this fascinating topic.

We might wonder how empathy differs from sympathy and compassion, as these three emotions are sometimes equated or misunderstood. Sympathy is feeling pity or sorrow for someone else's misfortune. It does not automatically include the aspect of sharing the emotions and feelings of the other person. As mentioned in chapter 4, compassion literally means "to suffer with another," feeling another's emotions and being willing to relieve that person's distress. A compassionate person would not necessarily attempt to understand the other's beliefs and experiences, as an empathic person would, but would try to take action to alleviate the suffering.

Roman Krznaric, a leading researcher on the subject of empathy, lists several habits that can help us develop empathy:

Become curious about strangers, and talk with them to learn about their lives. Take a moment to converse with others in line at the post office, in the doctor's waiting room, or at the ball game. Invite a new neighbor over for coffee or tea. I've struck up conversations with fellow travelers in airports and on planes and have learned about lives very different from my own. Martin Seligman, known as the father of positive psychology, says that being curious about others promotes greater life satisfaction.

Step into other people's shoes, even those with whom we disagree, and acknowledge their humanity and perspectives. This will challenge our prejudices, and empathizing with adversaries helps cultivate a more tolerant society. Take time to discover overlapping areas of interest with those who seem to have very different priorities and lives.

Listen carefully to others, and be fully present in the conversation. Silence your phone and put it out of sight. For heaven's sake, if you're talking to me and constantly checking your phone, you aren't paying much attention to what I'm saying. Nothing shouts, "You aren't very important!" like leaving your phone on the table and checking it every so often as we converse.

Be vulnerable. Take off your disguises and whatever roles you usually play and reveal your feelings gently. We connect with others most deeply when we share our imperfections and struggles.

Learn about people and cultures that are unlike your own. We can explore foreign worlds through art, literature, and film. Empathy is an essential part of human nature all over the globe.[60]

These suggestions provide guidelines in nurturing empathy throughout our lives. But we mainly learn it by watching how our actions affect other people, and we need immediate feedback to acquire the skill. This skill develops quite slowly, and not through looking at screens while texting or e-mailing. An analysis of seventy-two studies found that empathy declined among college students between 1979 and 2009. Students were less likely to take others' perspective and showed less concern for others.[61] Part of the reason for this growing empathy deficit in young people is most likely due to more screen time and less face-to-face interaction.

> ## PRACTICE
>
> Watch a foreign film or documentary with family or friends that illuminates a different culture. Imagine what it would be like to live in that country and consider all the ways we are more alike than different. Keep all cell phones in another room while you're watching, and talk about what you learned afterward. Such an event, with its accompanying conversation, can help develop skills of empathy.

Elevation is a term psychologists use to denote the emotional response that occurs when we see moral goodness in others. We feel warmth and appreciation for those individuals when we witness their empathic behavior. We are uplifted when we see a kind act, perhaps feeling joy for hours afterward. I experienced that a while ago when William, one of our young Guatemalan friends, needed a ride to the doctor for a required checkup. I was happy to volunteer and spend some time catching up with him, although the car ride would be a lengthy one. The journey entailed driving from the northern suburbs of Pittsburgh through the city to the southern suburbs, fetching William, heading north again to the doctor's office, and finally to the city center to drop him at his workplace. The commute would take place during the morning rush-hour traffic, and I was dreading the mayhem.

I began my travels around seven, bracing myself for the worst, but the expected bottlenecks of traffic became moments of disbelief: One after another, I witnessed drivers waving others into their lanes, cars slowing to help folks cross several lanes of traffic on a jam-packed bridge, patient commuters who used their horns solely for "your turn, go ahead" taps. By the time we arrived at the doctor's office ninety minutes later, dread was replaced with joy and amazement at the kind people of Pittsburgh. I also noticed how much this parade of kindness affected me, as I waved others into my lane with a smile on my face.

Days later, I was still delighted when recalling the goodwill I had witnessed. Elevation inspires us to carry that spirit of kindness forward, motivating *us* to act generously, too. One act, witnessed by others, can cause ripples affecting hundreds of people. A pebble dropped in a pond always creates ripples, and an act of kindness will do the same.

> If we are too busy to be kind, we are too busy.
> —Allan Lokos

One characteristic of elevation is that it is contagious. When we see kind acts, they seem to resonate deeply with us, and we are then inspired to be more loving, hopeful, and optimistic.[62] We are truly "wired to be inspired." It's in our genetic makeup. What makes us so powerfully affected when we see one human being helping another, particularly those who are strangers? Psychologist Jonathan Haidt notes that we want to live in a world where human beings treat one another with care and love. When we see a stranger perform a good deed for another stranger, it makes us think that maybe we *do* live in that world. Witnessing unexpected acts of kindness, compassion, and empathy motivates us to help others and become better people ourselves.

Social contagion, as this is called, is studied by Yale social scientist Nicholas Christakis. His research shows that if you become happier with your life, a friend who lives near you has a 25 percent higher chance of becoming happy, too.

> Kindness is in our power—even when fondness is not.
> —Samuel Johnson

Your partner will probably be happier as well. This happiness can also spread to people you barely know. "Just as some diseases are contagious . . . we've found that many emotions can pulse through social networks." . . . "Rather than asking how we can get happier, we should be asking how we can increase happiness all around us."[63] Each of us can spread joy around our world quite easily. Start with one act of kindness, and let the ripples of warmheartedness extend across your world.

As Alice Walker said so beautifully:

> Do you ever wonder . . .
> where so much love comes from?
> I wonder this often,
> because no matter how distressing the world is,
> wherever I am, there never seems to be a shortage of love.
> Is this true, as well, for you?

Last year, our oldest daughter Sarah saw a young Starbucks worker, dressed all in black with lots of body piercings, taking a break on the curb. The young woman was scrolling through her phone, looking tired, lonely, on the verge of tears. Another young woman around the same age walked up to the Starbucks girl. This other girl looked like your typical suburban schoolgirl: ponytail, Converse shoes, stylish clothes. The car next to Sarah's was filled with other suburban-looking girls waiting and smiling toward their friend. Sarah didn't hear anything but the end of the exchange, when the Starbucks girl said, "You have no idea how much this means to me. You just made my day."

That stopped Sarah in her tracks and filled her heart with peace. Then the two girls exchanged a hug.

When the other girl got into the car with her friends, Sarah jumped out of her car, tapped on their window, and said to them, "I'm not sure exactly what happened there. But I'm so impressed and proud of the young women you all are." They seemed to accept that from a thirty-five-year-old mom who was nervous to approach a car of teenagers. Sarah said that the incident created her new motto: "Don't stand by when you see goodness. Applaud it!"

PRACTICE

Remember: We never know how many ripples our little acts of kindness will produce. But kind acts are a first step in bringing healing to our world. Take a moment to think about the people in your life, perhaps someone who is struggling. Reach out to them this week with a friendly phone call or invitation to coffee. Simply offer your presence, even if only for a few minutes. It will brighten their day, and probably yours, too.

What small act can you do today to soften the harshness of our world?

I was the beneficiary of a very thoughtful act last year. My husband, Jack, and I had landed in Denver's airport and settled in for a two-hour layover, en route to a weekend conference. Noticing a woman nearby knitting a beautiful multicolored scarf, I wandered over to compliment her handiwork. "Joy" was happy to tell me about her project, sharing some details about her recent retirement and the new grandbaby she'd be visiting for the first time. One story led to another, and before we knew it, thirty minutes had passed and we were chatting like old friends. I mentioned that I would love to buy her scarf, but Joy said, "Absolutely not! I'll *give* it to you when it's finished!" Although I protested repeatedly, she insisted that it would be her pleasure to make it a gift.

Sure enough, a package arrived the following week containing the scarf, lovingly
swaddled in robin's-egg-blue tissue paper

> Be kind to one another.
> —Ephesians 4:32

with a sweet note inside from Joy. (And by the way, was anyone named more appropriately?) I love not only its beautiful colors and unusual shape but also, even more, the spontaneous generosity it represents.

Being on the receiving end of such a lovely gesture prompted me to contemplate the impact of kind acts like Joy's. Neuroscientists consistently preach that the primary antidote to feeling down in the dumps is to do something for another person. We humans are made for connection, hardwired to feel joy when we partake in, or simply witness, a loving action. We are healthier when we live with empathy and kindness: our immune systems are boosted, stress and inflammation are reduced, and our brains perform better. We are less likely to suffer from depression and heart disease. We do all this without seeking attention or hope of reward. Of course, Jesus taught this message over and over again: "Just as you did it to one of the least of these who are members of my family, you did it to me" (Matthew 25:40).

PRACTICE

Create a "Kindness Jar" for your family, in which each member deposits notes of kind deeds they witness or do themselves. At the end of the week, pull out the notes and share the deeds with the family. This practice will teach children not only to seek ways to express kindness but also to discover that sharing good deeds makes us happier and more loving.

When taking out the trash one night, I spotted my next-door neighbor Bill walking with our neighbor Bart. Bart is an adult with special needs. He has a cheery disposition and often wanders our streets looking for friendly conversation. Bill and Bart were deep in discussion, striding at a brisk pace, and the sight made me smile. It was good to see Bart joyful but also to witness Bill cheerfully welcoming Bart on his evening stroll. On a few occasions, Bart has commented to me that some neighbors turn the other way when they see him, which of course is hurtful. So to see him so engaged and happy made me happy! And to know that Bill was gladly giving the gift of time to our young neighbor brought me that warm feeling of "elevation," as I witnessed Bill's kind deed.

Although we may feel overwhelmed some days by all the suffering in our world, we can do our part to bring a bit of light to others. What we say and do matters, and it matters deeply. Our good deeds *are* important in a weary world. Researchers note that it is more psychologically rewarding to practice kindness in large chunks.[64] It's effective to pick one day a week to focus on being kind every way you can.

Our "unremembered acts of kindness and of love" are crucial in fashioning a more caring society for all of us. Perhaps one of the simplest ways to nurture empathy and

> Let everyone be quick to listen, slow to speak.
> —James 1:19

bring healing and light to our world is to share ideas with people. In this way, we create deeper understanding and stronger communities. As we listen to others, we honor them and build trust and better relationships. Radio host Celeste Headlee offers ten basic rules of good conversation, which serve as a framework to build healthy relationships.

- **Be fully present.** Don't multitask or let your mind wander off somewhere. And definitely put down your phone and look at the person!
- **Don't pontificate.** Psychologist M. Scott Peck said that true listening requires "a setting aside of oneself." You can learn

something from almost any person you meet, so no grandstanding or lecturing.

- **Ask open-ended questions.** Headlee suggests asking "who, what, when, where, and why" questions, since those simple questions can provoke more interesting responses.

- **Focus on listening.** When someone speaks to you, thoughts and stories will pop into your mind. Let them go and focus just on listening.

- **Admit it when you don't know something.** Honesty is always the best policy.

- **Don't equate your experience with the person speaking.** All experiences are individual. **Remember, it's not about you.**

- **Try not to repeat yourself.** It's condescending and boring.

- **Forget the details: the years, the names, the dates.** People don't care about details as much as they care about you and what you have in common.

- **The number-one most important skill is listening.** If your mouth is open, you're not learning. "Nobody ever listened his way out of a job," said U.S. President Calvin Coolidge.

- **Be brief.**

> Most people do not listen with the intent to understand; they listen with the intent to reply.
> —Stephen Covey

Listening to others: We have opportunities to practice our listening skills every single day. Review Headlee's suggestions and practice them with family and friends.

7

DISCOVERING
SELF-COMPASSION

"You shall love your neighbor as yourself."
—MATTHEW 22:39

We can have a negative reaction to the term *self-care*, because it sounds self-centered, even selfish. But self-care is actually a vital component of a healthy, happy, compassionate life. You may have been taught, as I was, that providing for the needs of others is a much more important pursuit than caring for ourselves. In fact, one of the most memorable songs from my Catholic school days is "They'll Know We Are Christians by Our Love." I could even belt out a few of its verses today, not that you'd want to hear it! The ideals I sang about are still deeply embedded in my psyche. However, I don't ever recall singing about loving ourselves. When I read the words in Matthew, "Love your neighbor as yourself," I recall the emphasis my teachers placed on the "neighbor" part of the quote, not on the "yourself" part. Why should we think about the "self" part of the equation? Because self-care increases our capacity to serve others and positively affects our families and communities. Self-compassion also supports our emotional and physical health, increases our resilience, and cultivates kindness and empathy toward others.

Let's be clear that when I use the term *self-care*, I don't mean to suggest you should book an expensive spa treatment at a local resort every weekend. I do mean practicing consistent, long-term, nurturing habits to sustain our lives of service. People sometimes avoid the habits of self-care because they are not glamorous. For example, when we eat a healthy dinner and get a good night's sleep. We can care for ourselves in various ways. Some examples include

- saying yes only to requests that you truly want to commit to and have the energy to fulfill;
- turning off the TV or streaming service to take a walk or go to bed at a decent hour;
- getting up early to pray, meditate, exercise, or slowly drink our morning coffee or tea;
- scheduling time for play and fun activities; and
- leaving ten minutes early for an appointment so the drive is stress-free.

Pick just one of these practices to incorporate into the next few days, and notice any difference you feel.

If we work nonstop without taking time for physical, psychological, and spiritual upkeep, we run the risk of serious burnout. How can we be good caregivers, chaplains, leaders, and teachers if we are tired, injured, or just plain worn out? The artist Julia Cameron reminds us, "If we don't give some attention to upkeep, our well is apt to become depleted, stagnant, or blocked."[65] If our wells run dry, we invite anxiety, depression, and a whole host of health problems into our lives. Our ability to serve others screeches to

> I will take care of myself for you, and you will take care of yourself for me.
> —Calvin & Hobbes

a halt. What kind of example does that provide to our children, friends, and colleagues when we run ourselves into the ground?

The latest research on self-compassion recommends several helpful practices, which came in handy as I recovered from minor knee surgery a while ago. I often soldier on when faced with difficulties, putting my head down and pushing through to the finish line. However, as Dr. Christopher Germer notes, it would be more fruitful to take a compassionate attitude toward ourselves, acknowledge the difficulties we are experiencing, and take time to care for ourselves with tenderness.[66]

The second night after my knee surgery, I was hobbling around the kitchen searching for something to eat. Exhausted and feeling a bit down in the dumps, I remembered one of Germer's exercises: recognize that things are difficult, and bring your hands to your heart. Take a few moments to breathe in and out. So, I sat down at the kitchen table, closed my eyes, and crossed my arms over my chest. This simple, loving gesture caused my body to release oxytocin, the feel-good hormone, which reduces stress and blood pressure. I sat with my arms across my heart, took several deep breaths, and after a few minutes, I felt much better.

There are two parts to this exercise, both of which are important: first, realize you are struggling, and next, give yourself a hug. This sounds so simple, yet it's very effective. Next time you're feeling overwhelmed, sick, or just sad, try this exercise. A short interlude like this may be all you need to recover some energy and perspective.

PRACTICE

Let's practice another self-compassion exercise now. Read the instructions below, and then close your eyes.

1. Hold your arms straight out from your shoulders and squeeze your fists as tightly as you can.

2. Think of a time when you were angry or upset. Hold for the count of ten.

3. Now relax your hands, turn your palms up, and then slowly bring your hands to opposite shoulders, crossing your arms over your heart. Think of someone who loves you very much. Hold for ten counts again.

4. Slowly release your arms and open your eyes.

You've just experienced what it feels like, emotionally and physically, to be bathed in anxiousness and then in self-kindness and oxytocin. How good it feels to remember that we are loved!

Dr. Kristin Neff, a prominent researcher on self-compassion, identifies its three components as self-kindness, common humanity, and mindfulness. Practicing self-kindness

> If your compassion does not include yourself, it is incomplete.
> —Jack Kornfield

simply means sending yourself kindness and understanding instead of judgment when things go wrong. When you make a mistake, be gentle with yourself instead of criticizing your failure and brooding about what you should have done, what you wish you had said, and so on. Give yourself a break, as you would for a good friend.[67]

For example, I recently forgot to pay a sales tax bill on time. The penalty was not small, and I felt terrible about wasting such a large amount of money. I began to berate myself for not remembering to put the deadline on my calendar. But I stepped back and asked myself, what good would that chastising do? Would it mean I would remember the deadline next year? Instead, I recalled how busy my life has been recently and how easy it was to forget a due date. Then I added a reminder in my calendar next year, so I wouldn't repeat the error. Dealing with a mistake in this manner was so much better than kicking myself endlessly for my blunder.

Richard Davidson, director of the Center for Healthy Minds at the University of Wisconsin–Madison, says, "Self-criticism can take a toll on our minds and bodies."[68]

It can lead to lying in bed at night replaying a difficult interaction, and it can interfere with our productivity. Self-criticism can also cause inflammation, ushering in chronic illness and accelerated aging. All these consequences can help motivate us to remember to go easy on ourselves. I've learned, finally, that life is too short to spend it regretting things we cannot change. We can let them go and move on. It's a much lighter way to live and frees up mental energy for important issues we can actually change.

The second aspect of self-compassion is recalling our common humanity. Suffering and failing are part of every person's human experience. None of us is perfect. We may hope to act flawlessly at all times, but that's impossible. If we expect perfection from ourselves, we are going to be disappointed pretty much every day of our lives. (And being around perfectionists is tiresome.) Being alone with disappointment is destructive because we isolate ourselves and make our suffering worse. Instead, it's important to keep in mind that every single person, no matter how perfect their lives may seem, makes mistakes on a regular basis. This attitude allows us to recover quickly from any blunders we make.

The third aspect of self-compassion is mindfulness, which simply means being aware of our emotions versus overidentifying with bad feelings. When we are mindful of our thoughts, we can more readily accept difficult situations as they occur. This increased awareness of negative emotions allows us to defuse them. We can acknowledge our mood, name it, and then let go of any troublesome thoughts. When I was limping around my kitchen on crutches after knee surgery, being mindful of my emotions gave me the insight to step back and take a few minutes to care for myself. If I had not taken a mindful moment, I would never have given myself the care I obviously needed.

Dr. Neff notes that when we practice self-compassion, several outcomes are likely: We find increased motivation and productivity, less depression and anxiety, more optimism, and greater happiness and life satisfaction.

PRACTICE

Self-talk is an important component of self-care, and paying attention to your internal thoughts and words is the first step toward a healthy mind-set. In the next few days, take time to notice your internal dialogue. What does that conversation sound like? Is your language affirming or critical? Do you talk to yourself more harshly than you would to a good friend? You may want to record any patterns you discover. These observations will help guide you in eliminating unhelpful thoughts and replacing them with gentle, affirming ones.

Dr. Chris Germer discusses five paths to self-compassion that can transform our lives: softening into the body, allowing our thoughts, befriending our feelings, relating to others, and nourishing our spirits. Let's explore each path and see how they build self-compassion.[69]

> Extending kindness to ourselves means we see ourselves as human beings who are wonderfully made by God and valuable, yet who are imperfect and make mistakes.
> —Kim Fredrickson

The first pathway is to "soften into the body," since taking care of our physical selves can clear our minds and give us much-needed physical rejuvenation. Often we tighten our muscles when under pressure, which can create musculoskeletal problems. This tightening sends signals to our brain that our body is in fighting mode, which doesn't help if we want to relax. Remember that an easy way to soften is to use your breath and relax your belly with each out-breath. Extend your exhalations longer than your inhalations, and you'll tamp down your nervous system. Then breathe into other tight parts of the body, and soften.

Movement can also clear our minds, and it's a practice I use regularly. Massage, stretching, yoga, or tai chi can loosen muscles. You might walk around the block. I sometimes do a few simple stretches when I need to be seated for extended periods.

Check in with yourself with these questions:

- Am I tired? Take time to rest or take a nap.
- Am I stiff? Stroll around the room.
- Are my neck and shoulders feeling tight? Time to do some neck rolls and shoulder shrugs.

When we notice what our bodies are telling us, we can respond with appropriate self-care.

Finally, one of the most powerful ways of being kind to ourselves is to forgo rushing around from morning till night, day after day. Catch yourself rushing, and pull back. Walk to the restroom extra slowly, making it a meditative break. When the phone rings, take two deep breaths before answering. Do whatever you know will ease your stress. How good it is to care for our physical needs by pausing to breathe, stretching our muscles, and not rushing throughout the day.

The second and third pathways address our thoughts and feelings. We allow thoughts to come and go, not holding on too tightly to anything upsetting or difficult. Remember that our evolutionary tendency to cling to unpleasant information helped our ancestors survive. But that tendency is often not helpful in today's world. Keep in mind the advice to treat bad news with a Teflon attitude and good news with a

Velcro attitude. Often, thoughts seem to have their own momentum, taking us along for a ride we don't seem to remember signing up for. In order to get off the train before it takes us to far-off destinations, ask, *Is this really important? Will I remember in a week, a month, a year?*

Another healthy self-care strategy is to acknowledge irritations and let them pass. We refrain from expending energy to suppress our emotions. We feel them fully and continue living in the present moment. It can be helpful to name your emotion, such as "Anger," "Irritation," "Disappointment," "Frustration." This gives us some psychological space from them. If we become agitated, elevated levels of stress hormones can weaken the functioning of our prefrontal cortex, or PFC. We lose our impulse control, our empathy, and our ability to see the big picture. The primal brain areas like the amygdala are strengthened, and our primitive brain winds up in control of our thoughts and emotions. That's when the tendency for inappropriate judgment and action increases. We may freeze up or "lose it" and act in ways we later deeply regret. Instead, we can stay with our emotions for a few minutes, identify them, and then choose an activity to lift our mood. We can take a walk, call a friend, listen to some favorite music, garden, bake, sing, or play a game—whatever brings a sense of calm.

The fourth pathway to self-compassion is relating to others and nurturing our relationships. Feeling lonely and marginalized is bad for our mental and physical health. In fact, research indicates that chronic loneliness is equivalent to smoking fifteen cigarettes a day, illustrating how important social ties are to our longevity.[70] Tending to relationships with family, friends, and neighbors means we are less likely to develop Alzheimer's disease, dementia, cardiovascular issues, and immune-system difficulties. Simply enjoying the company of others qualifies as self-care.

During the coronavirus pandemic, I discovered just how important it was to maintain relationships. I longed to connect with friends and family more than ever. But I rekindled old friendships, too, as I realized I'd neglected to actually talk, not text with them, for too long. Each and every conversation left me feeling renewed and joyful. The months of social isolation taught me that tending to my relationships truly nourished me.

Last, Germer invites us to cultivate the spiritual values we hold dear. He recommends noticing ordinary miracles, like hot water coming out of a spigot, paved roads that provide safe passage, and a warm bed at night. Other ways to support our spirituality are to attend services, read inspiring works, sit in silence, meditate, listen to music, garden, walk in the woods, and so on.

PRACTICE

Take a few moments today to ponder the ways in which you feel nourished: Is it a walk in the woods? Participating in church services? Visiting a friend? Reading an inspirational essay? Baking? Gardening? Playing piano? Listening to your favorite music or a meaningful podcast? Taking a class? Whatever it is that offers your body and soul some rest, take the time to do it before climbing into bed tonight.

When faced with a stressful situation, the Self-Compassion Break is quite helpful. It came in handy when a customer stormed out of my booth at a conference in Baltimore. The woman and I were having a heart-to-heart conversation about several topics, and because she was in a scooter, I asked about her disability. The woman flew into a rage, yelling at me, and rushed away. I felt terrible about hurting her, even though I was unsure what I had said that insulted her. I sat down in the back of my booth, closed my eyes, and walked myself through the following steps:

- First, I said to myself, *This is really difficult, and is a moment of suffering.* I noticed what was going on for me emotionally, just allowing the experience to be as it was.

- My next thought was reminding myself that suffering is a part of life, recognizing that my experience was not unique and that others suffer, too. I recalled that each of us might unwittingly make mistakes, causing pain to ourselves and others.

- Then I crossed my hands over my heart, felt the warmth of my hands and the gentle touch on my chest, and silently said, "May I be kind to myself. I did not intend to cause harm." I repeated these words several times for about ten minutes, calming my emotions, and offered a prayer of compassion for the woman.

I felt much better after taking this Self-Compassion Break and continued working the conference without berating myself anymore.

This portable exercise is useful anytime you feel agitated or distressed. You might consider saying other phrases, like "May I give myself the compassion that I need," "May I accept myself as I am," "May I be strong," or "May I be patient." If you practice in moments of relative calm, you may more easily experience the three parts of self-compassion—mindfulness, common humanity, and self-kindness—when you need them most. Positive self-talk helps us in several other ways, too. It reduces stress, increases our confidence and resilience, and aids in building better relationships.[71]

> Self-compassion is simply giving the same kindness to ourselves that we would give to others.
> —Dr. Christopher Germer

PRACTICE: A SELF-COMPASSION PAUSE

If you are struggling with a difficult situation, you might want to use this exercise to help cope with your emotions.

Think about a time when a close friend was going through a difficult time. What would you say or do for your friend in these situations? Perhaps jot down a few thoughts. Now think about times when *you* are struggling. What does your internal dialogue sound like? How do you talk to yourself? Are you supportive and encouraging, or critical and unsympathetic? The next time you are grappling with a difficulty, try treating yourself as you would treat a good friend and notice how much better you feel.

PRACTICE: SENDING KIND THOUGHTS TO OURSELVES AND OTHERS

Begin by closing your eyes. Sit tall, in a comfortable spot, with your feet on the floor. Cross your arms over your chest or choose another gesture that indicates loving-kindness.

Repeat these phrases silently: *May I be safe. May I be healthy. May my heart be at peace.*

After several minutes, call to mind a person you care about, someone who needs love and kindness in their lives, and repeat these phrases: "May she/he be safe. May she/he be healthy. May her/his heart be at peace."

Now, after several more minutes, think of another person whom you may not know well but who is hurting or suffering in some way. Repeat the same phrases for them: "May she/he be safe. May she/he be healthy. May her/his heart be at peace."

Now think of a person who may be causing you pain or suffering. Repeat the same phrases for them: "May she/he be safe. May she/he be healthy. May her/his heart be at peace."

If we begin sending good intentions to others regularly, these prosocial thoughts become embedded in our psyches. Our natural inclination is to care for others, and this quality deepens and widens the more we recite our intentions. Research indicates that practicing such a meditation that focuses on loving-kindness changes the brain and makes us more compassionate toward others. Dr. Richard Davidson and his colleagues found that incorporating a thirty-minute loving-kindness meditation for fourteen days caused an increase in the activity of the anterior insula cortex, the brain area associated with empathy. The subjects repeated phrases such as "May you have happiness. May you be free from suffering. May you experience joy and ease." At the end of the two weeks, the subjects' compassion for both themselves and others increased, as did their generosity.[72]

Loving-kindness meditations have had an effect on my daily interactions with others, particularly "anonymous" workers who serve me. I'm more likely to engage in conversation, take the time to learn more about their lives, and find points of connection. The world becomes a brighter, gentler place for all of us.

> Self-care is a radical act of love that increases my capacity for impact.
> —Shelly Tygielski

8

ENJOYING NATURE
AND AWE

On the glorious splendor of your majesty,
And on your wondrous works, I will meditate.
—Psalm 145:5

To walk in nature is to witness a thousand miracles.
—Mary Davis

A few years ago, my husband and I hiked the Tour of Mont Blanc, sleeping in huts and small hotels along the way. We were on our own in the Alps for ten days, navigating with a guidebook on the mostly well-marked trails. Many of the mountain paths were rocky and steep, crossing streams and valleys, so our attention was often fixed on the ground four feet ahead of us. Once or twice we took a wrong turn and had to retrace our steps to continue in the right direction. Other hikers were few and far between. It was the longest stretch of time I'd ever spent in the outdoors, and I experienced profound joy and peace. Silence was broken only by the wind rustling through trees, soothing sounds of rushing streams, and an occasional cowbell. We practiced what Rob Walker, author of *The Art of Noticing*, recommends to all of us: See the world instead of just looking, listen carefully instead of just hearing, and notice what matters to us, instead of just accepting what the world presents to us.[73] Without originally planning for it, we had tuned into the natural world in a deep way, inspiring profound gratitude for creation and the gift of life.

One of my favorite authors, the late neurologist Oliver Sacks, noted this about the effects of nature:

> [Most] of us have had the experience of wandering through a lush garden or a timeless desert, walking by a river or an ocean, or climbing a mountain and finding ourselves simultaneously calmed and reinvigorated, engaged in mind, refreshed in body and spirit. The importance of these physiological states on individual and community health is fundamental and wide-ranging.[74]

A Harvard Medical School report in 2018 summarized the many benefits of taking a walk in the natural world. It is a simple way to reduce stress, anxiety, and depression, and perhaps even to improve memory. Listening to the soothing sounds, or even the silence, in nature can lower our blood pressure and the levels of the stress hormone cortisol, calming the body's fight-or-flight response. Another study determined that the amount of time needed in nature to significantly reduce cortisol was twenty to thirty minutes, three times a week.[75] It made no difference whether the subjects sat or walked; they simply needed to spend time in a natural environment. The maximum benefit occurred during daylight, without electronic distractions such as cell phones. Other researchers found their subjects were more attentive and happier and had reduced cravings for smoking, excessive drinking, and overeating after being outside in green spaces.[76]

Mindful Walks in Nature

I occasionally take mindful walks in one of the wooded trails near our home. I stroll and simply take time to notice aspects of nature, as

Harvard psychology professor Ellen Langer recommends.[77] I look at the varied tree barks and the patches of new evergreens covering the forest floor; I listen to the chirping of birds and catch a glimpse of deer munching on brush in the distance. I spy bright red berries hanging from the bushes at the trail's edge, and the sky overhead filled with various cloud formations. There is so much to notice! I try to stay in "looking" mode and appreciate all these beautiful gifts of creation.

Neurologist Oliver Sacks notes:

> I cannot say exactly how nature exerts its calming and organizing effects on our brains, but I have seen in my patients the restorative and healing powers of nature and gardens, even for those who are deeply disabled neurologically. In many cases, gardens and nature are more powerful than any medication.

For years, I ran in these woods daily. My worn-out knees no longer accommodate running, but I can still walk through the tree-lined paths. Sometimes I forget how much happiness comes from being immersed in nature. One research study concluded that "participants showed significant increases in mood, well-being, mindfulness and meaning" and "the effect was stronger when participants spent at least thirty minutes in nature for thirty days."[78]

When we focus on pleasant surroundings like trees and greenery, our mind is distracted from negative thinking, so our thoughts are less filled with worry. These visual aspects of nature soothe our psyches, leading to less brooding. Researchers recommend retreating from urban settings for two hours a week:

> "People who spend at least 120 minutes in nature a week are significantly more likely to report good health and higher psychological well being than those who don't visit nature at all during an average week. . . . No such benefits were found for people who visited natural settings . . . for less than 120 minutes a week."[79]

The type of setting doesn't seem to matter, either. The goal is simply to get away from the city environment and surround yourself with a natural one.

Interestingly, those who aren't able to retreat to a natural setting can experience cognitive benefits just by looking at pictures of nature. Research indicates that viewing nature pictures lowers stress and improves attention.[80] Psychologists conclude that spending time in nature nurtures our health in a variety of ways. Wilderness therapy programs are also becoming more widely available. With Americans spending up to 90 percent of their time indoors, doctors are prescribing "doses of nature" to alleviate depression and anxiety.

PRACTICE: PRAYER TIME WITH NATURE

This week, try to sit in a natural setting where you can hear birds chirping, or the rustling of leaves, or perhaps a stream trickling through the woods. You may be able to hear nature sounds from your own backyard. Wherever you decide to sit, just focus your attention on a nearby sound. When your thoughts wander, simply return to the sounds. Stay for ten to twenty minutes, enjoying the soothing sounds of God's creation, a gift we so often ignore or forget.

We see that the gift of creation bestows many benefits. As we steep ourselves in this gift, we are in touch with God's wonders, as Scripture reminds us over and over again.

> Stop and consider the wondrous works of God.
> —Job 37:14

Natural environments capture our attention and are inherently compelling to us, probably because of evolution. Our cognitive control gets a break, restoring those resources, and our working memory improves. Nature also helps relieve depression, increasing our creativity and our ability to connect with others. In addition, the brain areas associated with empathy and altruism are activated when we view natural scenes.

What makes nature such a healing environment, bringing greater well-being and happier relationships? One possibility is awe, that feeling of wonder and amazement and of being in the presence of a higher power, says researcher Craig Anderson.[81] Sensing that we are a small part of this vast universe may allow us to feel that our worries and problems are less significant in comparison. Awe has two essential characteristics: vastness, as described above, and accommodation, which is the need to make sense of the monumental and extraordinary.[82]

Our feelings of awe, although uncommon, can be life changing. When awestruck, we perceive our personal concerns as insignificant in light of what psychologist Abraham Maslow called "peak experiences." He described episodes of awe as including "disorientation in space and time, ego transcendence and self-forgetfulness; a perception that the world is good, beautiful and desirable." He believed that epiphanies such as this could have profound effects, because awe teaches us that life can hold deep joy, wonder, and gratitude.[83]

Many of us experience awe as a spiritual and religious encounter. We might sense the presence of God as we look out over a magnificent view, like a picturesque sunset or a mountain range in the distance. Sometimes we are even rendered speechless when taking in these beautiful slices of creation. Anderson says, "Our study illustrates the importance of trying to find moments to enjoy nature and feel in awe of it. People need to learn to slow down and make space for that in their lives."

Scripture is filled with passages recounting the deep joy we can find in God's creation.

When I look at your heavens,
the work of your fingers,
the moon and the stars,
that you have established.
Psalm 8:3

You have made heaven, the heaven of heavens,
   with all their host, the earth and all that is on it,
     the seas and all that is in them. To all of them you give life,
     and the host of heaven worships you. (Nehemiah 9:6)

Let's look at a few ways that awe makes our lives better:

- Awe drops us into the present moment, and we experience an expanded sense of time, even if we see the imagery on a screen.

- Awe inspires creativity. It helps us think more flexibly and see things in a new light. Go outside or watch a nature video to get your creative juices flowing.

- Awe connects us to nature. Being filled with wonder and amazement are common responses to watching a powerful storm, a roaring river, or a beautiful sunset. Ralph Waldo Emerson said that in nature, "currents of the Universal Being circulate through me." We "sense the presence of a higher power," as researchers Keltner and Haidt note. So let's take the advice of the Christophers: "Happiness need not be pursued in exotic places. The joyful music of Creation surrounds us. All we need to do is listen."[84]

During a visit with our grandchildren in California, I volunteered to take two-year-old Sawyer to daycare one morning. We walked several blocks and arrived before the doors opened. To pass the time, we walked around the parking lot, spotting leaves in the puddles. She enthusiastically pointed out stems, veins, and colors in each leaf, picking up a few and delighting in each one. I can't recall the last time I looked at the details of ordinary leaves so intently. This is one gift of grandchildren: they teach us to see the ordinary with new eyes. How often I pass by leaves without even noticing their shapes and colors. Their elaborate beauty is always there to notice if we just take a few moments to do so.

We sometimes receive an even rarer glimpse into nature, as we did when a momma robin built her nest in the rhododendron bush outside our front window. It was the perfect spot for us to observe the mother bird feeding her hatchlings several times a day. We were enthralled as we watched the nestlings grow bigger by the hour.

One morning, however, I walked downstairs to check on "our" birds, and my heart sank: Disaster had struck! The nest was empty, and momma robin was nowhere in sight. I desperately looked around outside and found one of the fledglings lying on the ground, still breathing, but not moving much. I quickly went online to find out how we could rescue it. Turns out, you *can* return a bird to its nest without the mother rejecting it. My husband, Jack, grabbed his shovel and gently lifted the baby bird back into its little home. A few hours later, the momma robin returned to the nest, and began feeding her little one again.

> That which sustains the flower of the field, the circling series of stars in the heavens, the structure of dependability in the world of nature everywhere . . . all this and infinitely more in richness and variety and value is God.
> —Howard Thurman

Days later, the nestling began hopping around the branches of the bush, eventually flying away, leaving me with mixed emotions: thrilled to have seen a bit of nature up close, but sad to lose that intimate view of a momma bird and her baby.

PRACTICE

Go outside today and investigate a small piece of creation: a leaf on a branch, a spider's web in the corner, a raindrop on a ledge, a flower on the roadside. No matter where we live, a piece of nature is within reach if we just open our eyes and look. Sit and take a few breaths simply observing, amazed at the intricacies in front of you. You don't have to travel far to experience awe.

Every Wednesday night, I take out the trash for Thursday's garbage pickup. On a clear night, I stand and gaze at the twinkling stars and distant planets. I remind myself to savor the sight of these celestial bodies. What if they appeared only once in a thousand years?

Did you know that there's an app for observing the night sky? With Sky View Lite you can point your phone at the sky and watch names of constellations and planets appear as the phone scans space.

PRACTICE

Look up at the stars at night. Locate the moon, a few constellations, or planets. Just think about how far away those celestial bodies are from Earth. Dwell in amazement and awe.

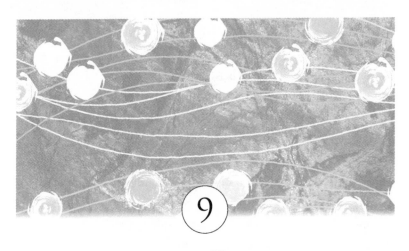

9

ENGAGING CREATIVITY
AND SOLITUDE

*There is something in every one of you that listens for the sound
of the genuine in yourself.*
—HOWARD THURMAN

*Learn to get in touch with silence within yourself and know that
everything in this life has a purpose. There are no mistakes, no
coincidences; all events are blessings given to us to learn from.
There is no need to go to India or anywhere else to find peace. You
will find that deep place of silence right in your room, your garden
or even your bathtub.*
—ELISABETH KÜBLER-ROSS

I grew up in a busy household of five children, and solitude wasn't
available without a determined effort. I loved wandering the nearby
woods or biking around our neighborhood with the wind in my face.
These excursions gave me a great sense of freedom, quiet time, space
to think, and deep-down joy. Today, hiking and biking still provide
tranquility and thinking time, particularly when I'm working on a
new design or writing a reflection. Psychologists, in fact, encourage us
to ponder the things we enjoyed doing when we were ten years old.

Participating in those childhood activities as adults will often bring happiness and spur creativity.

Solitude and creativity go hand in hand, because without solitude, our creative sparks will fade and die. Silence grounds creativity, birthing fresh ideas and original projects. These inspirations rarely arrive amidst the daily clamor of living, so holding time for incubation is essential. Novel thoughts can and do appear when the mind is still or aimlessly wandering without a goal in mind. This has been true for me, at least, for as long as I can remember.

PRACTICE

Close your eyes and bring to mind your ten-year-old self. Think of the everyday pursuits you really enjoyed. Linger on that for a while, then open your eyes. Write down one or more of those activities. Can you find a way to do that activity this week?

My postcollege professional life began at Gulf Research Laboratories in Pittsburgh, where I worked as an environmental engineer documenting the proper disposal of hazardous waste at the facility. It was not my dream job, to say the least. I was terribly bored, and every day I asked myself what I was doing there. Every morning I crossed the threshold of my office and began an hourly countdown. Months later, when I heard rumors of layoffs coming, I told my boss to feel free to let me go. I had no plans on continuing in engineering, and perhaps someone else's job could be saved. While waiting for the pink slip, I practiced calligraphy at my desk, never imagining that this skill would soon ground my life's work.

After leaving engineering, I dove headlong into studying calligraphy, buying books of lettering and practicing for hours on end. Along the way, I created a unique style of my own. I became an observer of design, finding it everywhere around me: magazines, newspapers, department store signs, gardens, museum placards, billboards, commercial print ads. I took note of what I liked and created a file to inspire my card designs. The quotes I'd been collecting since fifth grade were paired with my simple artwork, and a new journey had begun.

This journey has been anything but straight or predictable. In my sophomore year in high school, I filled out a form attached to a standardized test, listing academic strengths, interests, and expected profession. The printout, which I've kept all these years, notes scant artistic ability and a projected profession as a lawyer or engineer. There in black and white, I had all but eliminated the possibility of artistic expression in my adult life. But only a few years later, the beauty and craft of calligraphy drew me in, opening my eyes to design and an artistic side of me that I didn't know existed. To be in my fourth decade of creating is still a great surprise.

You might wonder whether creativity is inherited or learned, and it's actually a little of both. Children are born creative but often lose touch with it as they grow up.

George Land tested sixteen hundred children ages three to five, and then again at age ten and fifteen, and last, as adults. His results showed that creativity plummeted from 98 percent in five-year-olds to 2 percent when the test was given to 280,000 adults. Land concluded that noncreative behavior is learned.[85] Creativity can be nurtured and regained. Our creativity is waiting to be developed, as mine was. It also seems that the main determinant of creativity is our belief about ourselves. If you think you are creative, then you are freer to become creative.

We draw upon our creative muscles regularly in daily life, even though we might not name them as such. We plan parties and classes, choose music for special dinners or liturgies, arrange flowers in our vases and gardens, and write notes of condolence. Perhaps we have a room to redecorate or a vacation to plan. All of these draw upon our creativity in different ways, nurturing our brain health simultaneously.

I recently said to a customer, "Every one of us has creative abilities of one kind or another." She responded, "Well, I'm the kind that appreciates it!"

PRACTICE

Perhaps you might want to dip your toes in new creative waters but need a little push. Is there an art form you've always wanted to try? Maybe you're interested in painting with watercolors or crafting woodwork. Or you could sign up for voice or guitar lessons, attend a master gardening class, take a cooking or cake-decorating class. There is no limit to the variety of artistic endeavors available to us. Your local community college probably offers courses in many of these.

And finally, don't worry about skill. Let go of expectations and create unselfconsciously. Reconnect with the joy you found so easily as a child. Take a risk! You'll be glad you did.

Our best creative work occurs when levels of the neurotransmitters serotonin and dopamine are at high, but not excessively high, levels. Serotonin controls whether we are calm (high) or anxious (low). Proper levels of dopamine allow us to focus and maintain motivation, and stave off boredom, which occurs when levels are too low. We want to be "calm but energized" to maximize our creativity.[86]

> A spark of Divine Light is within each of us.
> —Pope Francis

One path for boosting our creativity is to spend time near a body of water, which benefits our physical and mental health, too. Sitting at the beach or the edge of a stream, or swimming in a lake can make us happier, help us sleep better, feel less stressed, and be more creative. Perhaps this is why 80 percent of the world's population lives within sixty miles of a body of water or a coastline. Human beings experience tranquility from the combined sights and sounds of water, experiencing reduced depression, anxiety, symptoms of PTSD, and addiction.[87] Some scientists who study how water affects us note shifting brain waves in those who relax and float in water. It seems that more active brain waves change to theta brain waves, which are associated with sleep and deep meditation. These slower brain waves help us learn, remember, access intuition, and stir creativity. Being near water is good for us in many ways.[88]

Other suggestions for enhancing our creativity include the following:

Get rid of stressors. The hormone cortisol blocks the effect of serotonin and rises with stress, so it behooves us to manage our stress levels. If you tend toward perfectionism, give that up as soon as possible. Trying to be perfect creates stress and, in case you haven't noticed, is impossible to achieve.

Get sleep. Lack of sleep has a negative effect on the brain's response to serotonin. Good sleep habits also help maintain our telomeres, so aim for seven to eight hours per night. The subconscious mind can solve problems and be creative during slow-wave sleep (about 20 percent of our sleep time) even though we're not conscious of the process. When this implicit system is at work, far-flung corners of the brain communicate with one another. By filling your brain with new ideas and inspiration before going to bed, your mind may come up with novel ideas while you're asleep. The saying "Sleep on it" is excellent advice. Creativity depends on those networks putting together information in new ways.

Protect your mornings. Work quality and creativity are often best in the morning hours when serotonin levels tend to be highest. Since proteins in the body are converted to serotonin and dopamine, try to eat a high-protein breakfast to maximize that benefit. Caffeine will magnify your emotions, so it can be helpful if it energizes you. If you're nervous, it's best to forgo it.

Fashion your workspace to augment creativity. Perhaps fill it with meaningful objects, but avoid overdoing it. Find a chair that is comfortable. Control the clutter; some people need a clean desk to work, and others need files and other resources close at hand. If it helps, repaint the space in a color that feels better for thinking and dreaming.

Search for inspiration and absorb. Look at art. Listen to music. Go into nature: Listen to grasshoppers, the wind, leaves rustling, raindrops. Tour a museum. Sit in a beautiful building with high ceilings, since they encourage abstract thinking. Keep a notebook at hand to jot down ideas. In the words of Jules Renard, "If I had my life to live over again, I would ask that not a thing be changed, but that my eyes be opened wider."

Exercise. Regular cardiovascular exercise releases a peptide that helps produce serotonin. Walk before or during a meeting, and that should increase ideas. Exercise also helps maintain and lengthen telomeres. Aim for forty-five minutes, three times per week.

Both positive and negative emotions can drive creativity. Watch an inspirational documentary. Read a moving story. Surround yourself with positive people. Choose silence or the music that helps you.

Keep interested and curious. Diversifying experiences help people break their cognitive patterns. These are also good for your brain health, too. Read and talk to others in different disciplines. Travel to a new destination. Attend a concert with unfamiliar music. Push your comfort zone. Habituation and stagnation are creativity killers. Learn to juggle or speak another language. Drive a different way to work, make your sandwich differently, stir the pot with your nondominant hand, stand on one foot while cooking, walk backwards. Relearn a childhood skill. Whatever activity you choose, it must be active, not vicarious, to increase cognitive flexibility.

Set internal restrictions. What can I do with what I have? For example, make a dish with only five ingredients. Create a painting with only three colors. Clean a room using only water, vinegar, and baking soda. I design my greeting cards in just two colors because of cost limitations, but I've found this helps focus my design work. Dr. Seuss used only fifty different words in *Green Eggs and Ham*, after his editor bet him he couldn't write a book using fewer than the 225 words used in *The Cat in the Hat*. Kierkegaard once said, "The more a person limits himself, the more resourceful he becomes."

Create distance and step away from the problem. When you encounter difficulty in your creative work, put it completely out of your mind and do something that energizes you. This incubation time is essential and highly effective. Daydream, reflect, or nap after you've done a bit of work.

Minimize interruptions. Put away your phone and silence distractions. Close tabs on your computer. Notify coworkers or family that you need uninterrupted time. If needed, use headphones to pipe in music or ambient sounds.

Stir your creative juices. Subconscious creative processes are aided by walking, skiing, snowshoeing, biking, gardening, swimming. Try to incorporate one or more of these into your days a few times each week, even if it's only for a short time. You may find, as I do, inspiration popping out of thin air during these repetitive activities.

My coworker Laurie arrived at the office one day with an article titled, "The Psychological Benefits of Baking for Other People." There is something deeply satisfying about whipping up a tasty treat and offering the results of our creativity to others, who gratefully welcome, then gobble

> Each of us is an artist of our days; the greater our integrity and awareness, the more original and creative our time will become.
>
> —John O'Donohue

up, the finished product. Never mind how good a kitchen or home smells when someone is busy baking. Mmm mmm!

I loved baking cookies as a young girl. My three brothers and sister would devour whatever I baked, even if it was a slightly burned pile of sugar, eggs and flour. Watching them eat my creations made me feel useful and appreciated. Plus, baking was a wonderful diversion on rainy days. Our house would fill with the aromas of chocolate chip cookies, and we would steal spoonfuls of cookie dough when my mom wasn't looking.

Because many of us bake for special occasions or as a hobby, we might enjoy knowing its psychological benefits. Ponder these thoughts the next time you decide to create a few goodies in your kitchen.[89]

Baking allows for creative expression. And it's well known that creativity enhances our well-being. Self-expression through baking is a stress reliever.

Baking is a form of communication. Sometimes there are no words to adequately express our gratitude, appreciation, or sympathy, but our gift of baked goods can wordlessly communicate our care and love.

Baking is a mindful activity, requiring your attention and focus. You have to measure, mix, stir, and sometimes even roll out the dough. "If you're focusing on smell and taste, on being present with what you're creating, that act of mindfulness in that present moment can result in stress reduction," explains Donna Pincus, professor of psychological and brain sciences at Boston University.[90]

Baking can ease unhappy thoughts. While you're creating a sumptuous treat, you concentrate on each step of the process, staying anchored in the moment. There isn't mental space available for ruminating, which can lead to depression and sadness. Engaging in a productive activity like baking produces a tangible reward to share with others, and that makes us feel good about ourselves.

Giving our baked creations to others is an altruistic act, and altruism has several benefits of its own, such as releasing "feel good" hormones and experiencing the self-satisfaction of knowing you've done something to help another. It lessens stress and may distract you from your own problems, even contributing to your life span; studies show that volunteers live longer than nonvolunteers.

And finally, in the words of Julia Child, "A party without cake is just a meeting."

If you find baking stressful or an unpleasant chore, you may not experience these psychological gains. As Professor Pincus says, "As long as it's not stressful and not obligatory, it can be beneficial for all."[91]

PRACTICE

Set aside an hour or two and create something in your kitchen. It doesn't have to be fancy or complicated. Perhaps bake a loaf of bread or a batch of cookies for your family, neighbor, mail carrier, or someone recovering from an illness or injury. If creating something from scratch sounds intimidating, get a boxed mix and just add water and eggs. Simply set an intention to be mindful in every step of the process: assembling the ingredients, measuring, pouring, mixing, stirring, setting the oven temperature, and finally retrieving the final product from the oven and arranging goodies on a platter. Who doesn't feel a sense of accomplishment at the end of a baking interlude?

My friend Ann works in a busy office in St. Louis, coordinating communications for an international religious community. Her husband retired recently, and they found it necessary to negotiate their daily

> In a good marriage each person appoints the other to be the guardian of his solitude.
> —Rainer Maria Rilke

schedules and expectations. Jim is ready to chat as soon as Ann walks through the door after her workday, but she needs a period of quiet time to recharge and restore her internal equilibrium. After attending a retreat that featured a coloring exercise, Ann decided to forge a new postwork habit. Now when she returns home, she quickly greets Jim, then heads upstairs to sit still and let go of the day's busyness. She meditates and colors a page or two, sometimes for an hour. This exercise in creativity and stillness brings calm to her spirit and resets her energy, allowing her to be more present to Jim afterwards.

Coloring and the Brain

The act of coloring can be effective in releasing stress and calming our nervous systems. Neuroscientist Stan Rodski notes that when the brain creates patterns through repetition and boundaries, such as coloring inside lines, it relaxes. Furthermore, when creativity is expressed in a noncompetitive way, the brain is calmed even more. Coloring is perfect, then, for settling anxious thoughts and staying in the present moment. This is true for 98 percent of us. The other 2 percent, who may have unpleasant childhood memories associated with coloring, find the activity stressful.

PRACTICE: COLORING PROJECT

- **Create a quiet space to settle in.** Light a candle or drop some essential oil onto a cotton ball to add a gentle scent to your space.
- **Coloring is a no-judgment zone.** You will not be graded on it, and you will receive no criticism. Just be free to go where you will.
- **Choose colors that speak to you and supplies that you enjoy using.** I'm partial to coloring pencils, and lots of them. It's possible to create lots of shades by varying the pressure and density of the strokes, even layering a few colors to create a new shade.
- **Take a moment or two to breathe after completing a small section.** Count four for the in-breath, six for the out-breath.

God created us to be creative! In *Things Hidden: Scripture as Spirituality*, Richard Rohr reminds us: "God wants images of God to walk around the earth . . . who can bear the darkness and the light, who can hold the paradox of incarnation—flesh and spirit, human and divine, joy and suffering, at the same time. Just as Jesus did."

Practicing mindfulness is a proven way to cultivate "incubation" and insight while building cognitive flexibility. By coming fully into the present moment and taking

> Be still, and know that I am God!
> —Psalm 46:10

mindful breaks throughout the day, we turn off the "autopilot" in our brain, allowing us to focus attention on the task at hand. Meditation is also helpful to our creativity, since research shows we are more open to original ideas after even a brief meditation period.

PRACTICE: FIVE STEPS TO THE CREATIVE PROCESS

1. **Focus your attention and prepare.** This is the stage where you gather material and absorb information related to your task. Usually this is best done in a quiet atmosphere.
2. **Incubation time, when all the ideas you've gathered sit in your subconscious.** Patience is important, and this fallow time is central to the process.
3. **The aha moment.** Often this moment occurs out of the blue when you're performing a low-level task like folding laundry, taking a shower, driving a car, taking a walk.
4. **Evaluation.** Ask yourself and others, "Is this really a good idea?" It's a very important step.
5. **Do the work.** This is the 99-percent-perspiration part. Put your nose to the grindstone and work on the project you've set for yourself.

My go-to method of stirring creative juices is to hike in the nearby woods and enjoy the solitude. By solitude, I refer to the definition in *Lead Yourself First*, coauthored by Raymond Kethledge: freedom "from inputs from other minds." This means that if you're out in nature and listening to a podcast or talking on the phone, you aren't experiencing solitude. It means time away from *all* human inputs. Daily doses of solitude are incredibly nourishing for mind, body, and spirit. When I walk on a pine-scented path, letting my mind wander, observing the towering trees, cloud shapes, red berries, and occasional deer, I come back completely refreshed. I think I'd find it impossible to handle my professional responsibilities without this grounding contemplative habit.

If you don't have a park or woods nearby, take a walk along the street, pausing to look at the details in your neighborhood: the sidewalk, porches, nearby buildings, and

> Pay attention not to what you are, but to *that* you are.
> —*The Cloud of Unknowing*

storefront displays. Look up at the sky and watch the clouds, taking in the changing colors and shapes above your head. Study people's faces and appreciate the variety found in the human beings you encounter. I sometimes wander into houseware stores just to admire the textures, shapes, and colors of plates, napkins, glassware, towels, chairs, utensils, etc. You'll find a plethora of patterns and colors to behold. Leave your phone at home and enjoy the visual bounty.

Many times I've biked in the park or walked in the woods and returned with a problem solved, an idea for a card design, or a creative retreat activity. Occasionally, a solution to a problem I wasn't even thinking about will pop into my head. Silence nourishes our brains, and in moments of solitude, we are evaluating and internalizing information. Even at rest, our brains are highly active. Two hours of silence per day has been shown to prompt cell development in the hippocampus, the brain region related to the formation of memory involving the senses. Because of our smartphones, many of us don't experience even a minute of solitude throughout the day, a phenomenon unheard of just ten years ago. We can only imagine what is being lost due to this hyper-connectedness. If internal and external noise is humming all around, inspiration will be elusive. What creativity has the world missed because of this incessant distraction?

PRACTICE

Choose to be alone for at least five minutes a day and see how solitude changes you.

The final word comes from Dr. Ruth Richards, one of the researchers who coined the term *everyday creativity*. She is a psychology professor at Saybrook University

Do not be afraid to dream of great things.
—Pope Francis

and Harvard Medical School, and she says that "engaging in creative behaviors makes us more dynamic, conscious, non-defensive, observant, collaborative, and brave." Creativity provides opportunities to flourish, making us "more resilient, more vividly in the moment, and, at the same time, more connected to the world."[92] When we nurture creativity, we nurture our "dreams of great things."

10

DEALING WITH DISTRACTION AND TECHNOLOGY

God may be calling you, but probably not *on your cell phone.*
—CHURCH SIGN

One Tuesday night, I drove the usual way home through a large county park. It's a ten-minute drive, and I called my mom to catch up. I was chatting away and made the left turn at the light, then immediately heard a siren and saw the flashing lights of a police car behind me. I pulled over, completely confused as to why I was being stopped. The officer walked to the window and asked, "Do you know what you just did?"

"No, I stopped at the light, then turned. Was just talking with my mom on my way home."

He said, "You ran a red light."

"What? I thought the light was flashing red, so I stopped, looked both ways, and continued on."

"No, the light was not flashing, so you weren't paying attention. You were distracted by your conversation." He let me go with a warning, advising me to keep my phone in my purse when I'm driving.

My embarrassing story demonstrates that our attentional skills are not as keen as we think they are. We live in an incredible time, with palm-sized technology able to function better than a room-sized computer could have a few decades ago. But this great gift comes with drawbacks and downsides that we are just beginning to sort out. Those of us who use technology regularly know firsthand that it can get in the way of intentional living. Probably all of us are familiar with the experience of searching the Web to find an answer to a simple question. We type in the subject, then up pops a breaking news story, then an urgent email, followed by a link to an interesting article, only to realize forty-five minutes are gone and we still haven't found an answer to the question that started the whole process. We may have forgotten what the question was to begin with!

Our devices bring us a wealth of information, allow us to compute complex problems, and provide entertainment that was previously unavailable to the average Jane. We can type an email to almost anyone in the world, and the recipient can respond within minutes, while the mail program helpfully points out a typo, saving us time and perhaps embarrassment. We share photos with family and friends far and wide, and FaceTime with them, too. We send funds across the miles without ever opening our checkbooks.

However, we need to ask ourselves if we are making conscious choices about how, and how long, we interact with our amazing technology. Research shows that we check our phones up to 150 times a day. That's every six to seven minutes we are awake! By one estimate, Americans spend almost eleven hours a day interacting with some form of screen.[93] Luckily for us, there are now apps that track screen time so we can monitor our usage. But more on that later.

Information Seeking in Today's World

Did you know that

- Nearly 40% of high schoolers text/e-mail while driving

  https://www.teendriversource.org/teen-crash-risks-prevention/distracted-driving

- 80% reach for the phone as soon as they wake up:

  https://blogs.constantcontact.com/smartphone-usage-statistics/

- *26% of teens say they text while driving

- *Texting while driving is responsible for at least 18% of deaths due to car accidents

- *23% of all car crashes involved cell phone use (* from The Distracted Mind, 130)

- 46% of young adults would prefer to break a bone to breaking their phone. https://www.forbes.com/sites/pauladavislaack/2018/11/16/ break-your-bone-or-break-your-phone-dealing-with-technology-stress/#2320ad e95af6

- The National Highway Traffic Safety Administration estimates nearly 3,500 people died in distraction-related crashes in 2015, and the problem may be worsening.

- Just a two-second distraction increases your risk of crashing by 20 percent.

- https://www.wired.com/2017/04/ turns-horrifying-number-people-use-phones-driving/

Why are we so drawn to these devices, so much so that some put their very lives at risk?

I own a smartphone, a smart TV (which seems to require a tech assistant to operate), a Mac computer, an Apple Watch, and an Amazon Echo. These devices possess great features, and we would be foolish to ignore all the advantages. But don't we need a healthier relationship with technology? And the important question is this: What are we giving up in exchange for hours online?

Remember, neuroscience teaches us that what we do and what we don't do affects our brains. We grow new connections and pare old ones based on what we practice, and these changes occur throughout our lifetimes. With this in mind, it's important to know that our brains are designed for information seeking. Our ancestors stayed alive in the forests and wilderness by collecting information about their environment. Every time they discovered a new, crucial detail that would help them find food, and therefore survive, they received little hits of dopamine. A gatherer might have encountered some plump purple berries and asked, "Can I eat them, or will they poison me?" Information was critical for their existence, and the "feel-good" neurotransmitter dopamine was released with every new piece of information.

What is dopamine? It's the hormone triggered when we anticipate a reward, and it's associated with euphoria and bliss. When dopamine sends signals to nerve cells, we feel good and experience a surge of energy. Every incoming message and ping brings new information and a bit of dopamine, and that's why it feels so good to constantly check our phones. Our behavior is rewarded and reinforced. We are foraging for information, as our ancestors foraged for food, and we shouldn't scold ourselves for being so attracted to it. We check our phones, receive a notification, then get a dopamine hit. Every time we get that reward, the connections between those particular neurons in our brains become stronger. With each positive stimulus, the release of dopamine reinforces the behavior that caused it. Dings and pings and notifications constantly interrupt our concentration and focus, resulting in decreasing attention spans and a loss of the ability to focus and remember.[94] But we should stop blaming technology and smartphones for that loss of attention and focus. This is how our brains evolved so we could survive.

This information-seeking part of our brain is very strong, much stronger than the "cognitive control" part that allows us to complete tasks. What is cognitive control? It is the brain structure that helps us make decisions based on our goals and not simply on impulses, habits, or reactions. Our cognitive control abilities have not evolved to the same level as the functions required for goal setting. We want to achieve goals, but we just love those little hits of dopamine. There is a mismatch between our information seeking and our cognitive control. We may decide to spend less time on our phones but find it incredibly difficult to disconnect. And now you know why.

When our cognitive control fails to thwart our tech overuse, we find several issues that must be addressed. First, if I'm socializing with family, friends, or coworkers and see someone checking their phone frequently, I get the impression the person doesn't care about us as much as about her incoming messages. It's possible those messages are of grave importance, but most likely they aren't. This lack of attention and empathy has long-term consequences for the quality of our most important relationships. In addition, an absence of ability to focus our attention leads to decreases in productivity and overall mental capabilities.

Imagine your attention is a beam of light emanating from a flashlight in your hand. You want to illuminate an object ahead, but another interesting object grabs your attention, so you flash the light beam on that. Then you remember to hold the beam on the intended object, but then another fascinating object grabs your attention. That's what it's like when our mind wanders and is unable to stay focused on the intended object. The light bounces all over the wall, chasing distractions and shiny objects instead of holding still on one thing.

"The ability to pay attention to important things—and to ignore the rest—likely helped early humans survive and evolve. Now, it's a skill that can help children and adults alike succeed in school, at work, and in their relationships."[95]

Another issue we need to consider is multitasking. Many people believe they can multitask, accomplishing two things at once. It feels good to imagine we're accomplishing a lot, and it feeds our emotional need for new and exciting tasks. However, the brain does *not* multitask but instead switches back and forth from one task to another, losing speed with every task change as it takes several minutes to regain full concentration.[96] This is not an efficient way to work because it slows brain processes and increases errors. "Multitaskers are 'suckers for irrelevancy,' which hampers not just concentration but also analytic understanding and empathy," note Goleman and Davidson.[97]

Dr. Sophie Leroy of the University of Washington dubs the cognitive cost from this constant checking and switching between tasks "attention residue." For example, if I'm writing an essay and I hear a *ping* and look at my phone to read a text message, it will take time to refocus when I return to writing the paper. The time it takes to adjust my focus—the residue, as Dr. Leroy named it—gets continually compounded throughout the day. Our attention is splintered, our stress and fatigue increase, and our performance suffers.

Multitasking also lessens our cognitive control, making us less able to resist distractions and more prone to making errors. We go round and round as our phones disrupt our concentration with beeps and buzzes, and we grow less capable of focusing on the tasks at hand. Assignments take longer to finish as these distractions send us off course. That's a genuine problem, not only for accomplishing mentally demanding tasks but also for our brains' prefrontal cortex, the area of the brain harmed by constant distraction.[98] Our critical skills of analysis weaken, along with the relational attribute of compassion.

It's important to know that the multitasking I'm referring to includes two or more tasks that require some brain cells to fulfill. It does not include an activity like folding laundry, which can easily be completed while watching an enjoyable TV program or chatting on the phone. Since many of our household tasks require very little cognitive bandwidth, you can fully engage in another task that requires your attention. But we might want to "monotask" household chores occasionally, using the chores as a mindful break in the day.

PRACTICE

This week, become more attentive to your cell phone use. Do you keep it on the table when eating with others? Are you checking it several times every hour? Just become conscious of how you are using technology, as that is the first step toward developing healthier habits. You may also find your stress levels decline, and that's a good thing, because chronic stress is associated with more errors and safety issues, concentration difficulties, and working-memory problems. Stress also inhibits our problem-solving skills and our attentional abilities. Going offline every so often, even daily, if possible, allows us to hold on to our sanity.

Human beings are extremely sensitive to distractions and interruptions. We cannot sustain attention and hold information while we engage in other demanding tasks, because we are easily distracted and interrupted. There is tension between what we'd like to do and what we can do. We try to set our sights on goals, focus on important tasks, and ignore distractions so we can accomplish those goals. This selective attentional skill is significant, and the act of ignoring is more important than most realize. It is a very active process requiring resources to filter out irrelevant info.

> The beauty of the digital age is we can make contact with people on the far corners of the earth. The challenge is we sometimes lose contact with ourselves, especially our deeper selves.
>
> —Pico Iyer

The skills of focusing and ignoring are two different processes. When we focus on a task, we're not necessarily ignoring distractions. We use neural resources when disregarding irrelevant information, and those resources are not infinite. You may have noticed that you aren't able to concentrate as well in a noisy coffeehouse as you did ten or twenty years ago. That's because older adults are more distractible than younger adults. Why? Because the prefrontal cortex, the area responsible for executive functioning and cognitive control, is one of the first areas to show signs of degradation as we age. Older adults do as well as twenty-year-olds for taking in relevant info but suffer deficits when ignoring irrelevant info.

We are sensitive to this interference because of our brain's limitations. Why is this important? With constant interruptions and distractions, which we try to ignore, our productivity decreases, as does our quality of life. Consequently, our brains change, and not for the better. We may try to engage with these interruptions and carry on, but our processing speed and accuracy decline.

Cognitive control is worst in young children. Then it steadily matures, peaking in our early twenties. This is immediately followed by decline as we approach middle age, then a steeper decline in the senior years. Long-term, short-term, and working memory decline as we age, as does processing speed. But the good news is that our verbal knowledge increases with age, with small declines coming after age seventy.

Long-term studies on older brains show that we grow smarter in key areas of our brains from middle age to our mid- to late sixties. Inductive reasoning ability increases, which means we draw conclusions from observations and connect disparate information better. We get the gist of arguments more readily, and our judgment of others improves. As we get older, our amygdala also reacts less to negative things. A new series of fascinating studies suggests that the way our brains age may give us a broader perspective on the world and the capacity to see patterns, connect the dots, even be more creative. We could say that we grow in wisdom.[99]

App engineers design their products to hold our attention and keep our eyeballs on their creations. There are all sorts of features embedded in online games and apps that entice us to spend more time on them. We get pings, "likes," and streaks, all of which help sell more ads and increase revenue for the app companies. They are making piles of money from our inability to block out these distractions.

"Making yourself inaccessible from time to time is essential to boosting your focus."[100]

A 2017 survey from the American Psychological Association found that being constantly and permanently reachable on an electronic device—checking work emails on your day off, continuously cycling through social media feeds, responding to text messages at all hours—is associated with higher stress levels.[101] [102]

Many parents in Silicon Valley, the very people who design our tech devices, carefully limit their children's use of cell phones and other technologies. They know quite well that these devices lead to attention declines and thwart the growth of beneficial neuronal connections in their children's developing brains. One activity many parents provide to nurture these young brains, and restore attention, is outdoor play in nature. Enjoying creation is like giving your brain a deep-tissue massage. The type of nature setting doesn't seem to matter. Dr. Jason Strauss, an instructor in psychiatry at Harvard Medical School, says, "The goal is to get away from stimulating city urban settings and surround yourself with a natural environment."[103] When we get outside, we give our cognitive control a break, restoring those resources, and improve our working memory and attention spans.[104] It isn't called the "great outdoors" for nothing.

Simply put, spending time outdoors makes people happier and decreases rumination and brooding. The prescribed amount of time to get away from urban settings is twenty to thirty minutes, three days

> I go to nature to be soothed and healed, and to have my senses put in order.
>
> —John Burroughs

a week, or spending a three-day weekend in the woods. So, if you want to improve your focus and attention easily, just take a walk along a tree-lined path.[105]

Scripture is filled with descriptions, like the one below from Psalms, of nature and its gifts. It reminds us to stop, look around, and enjoy this creation that has been bestowed upon us.

> Let the heavens be glad, and let the earth be rejoice;
>   let the sea roar, and all that fills it;
>   let the field exult, and everything in it.
> Then shall all the trees of the forest sing for joy.
>
> —Psalm 96:11–12

PRACTICE

Find a patch of forest or trees and take a walk. Be sure to use your sense of smell to catch whiffs of pine or cedar. Walking in nature not only keeps our brains healthy but, due to phytoncides emitted from trees, our immune systems are enhanced. Phytoncides are organic compounds that trees use to protect themselves from pests and diseases, with antibacterial and antifungal properties. When we breathe them in, they boost our immune systems, killing tumor- and virus-infected cells in our bodies. What's more, this positive effect can last for up to thirty days.[106] Just knowing those few positive effects of nature might motivate us to head outdoors more often. Our stress levels fall, our bodies become stronger, and we are happier.

Brief mental breaks, like walking in nature or viewing nature photos, are crucial to maintain our focus and energies when engaged in longer tasks. It is important to realize, though, that all breaks are not created equal. Here are a few research-based breaks that are restorative and stress reducing, adapted from Gazzaley and Rosen, *The Distracted Mind*, page 228.

> Overloading attention shrinks mental control. . . . Life immersed in digital distractions creates a near-constant cognitive overload.
>
> —Daniel Goleman

Exercise. A strong body equals a strong brain. As little as twelve minutes a day can improve attention and brain function. One exercise session will make our cognitive control measurably better. Many studies have shown the cognitive benefits of physical exercise in older adults.

When working at your computer, every twenty minutes, take a twenty-second break and focus on an object twenty feet away. This simple exercise will bring blood flow to brain areas you aren't using for attention.

Daydream, doodle, or do anything that takes you away from the specific task at hand. Since I often work at home, I'll go to my kitchen and do a few dishes, cut up fruit or veggies, or throw a load of laundry into the washer. A ten-minute break restores my lagging attention and helps me refocus on the task.

Sleep. I might sound like a broken record, but get your sleep. Just one bad night can impair cognitive control. Over the long haul, consistent sleep deprivation harms both your health and your brain. A ten-minute nap will improve cognitive function. Thirty-minute naps are helpful, too.

Talk to a human being. Yep. That will improve your work functioning and reduce stress. Of course, pick a person with whom you enjoy conversing. Some folks drain our energy, so choose wisely.

Laugh. Watch an amusing video. Look at a few comics. Your cortisol levels will decrease; endorphins and dopamine will increase. You'll feel less stress and have more energy and positive feelings.

The good news is that there are spiritual practices we can incorporate into daily life that will help restore these diminishing skills. The most effective one is meditation or silent prayer. Volumes of research indicate that meditation improves cognitive control, attention, processing speed, and working memory. (The latter three are the ones most sensitive to interference.) Taking time to still the mind will also increase our compassion for others and boost the electrical activity in the left side of the brain, the command center for our immune systems. This increased activity fortifies the immune system, producing more defense cells. Meditation also relieves stress, lowers blood pressure, and lifts one's mood. It seems that two hours of silence per day prompts cell development in the hippocampus, the brain region related to the formation of memory involving the senses. Just two weeks of meditation practice improves focus and working memory, and decreases the tendency to mind-wander.[107] And meditation seems to slow brain atrophy due to normal aging.[108]

Attention and working memory are better in people who meditate, and long-term meditators who are fifty to sixty years old outperform twenty-year-olds in visual attention skills. We also know that meditation builds cognitive reserve, which seems to delay the onset of neurological diseases such as Alzheimer's.[109]

When beginning a meditation practice, it's important to choose an amount of time that feels right for you. It's better to commit to a five-minutes-every-day time of silence, as opposed to a once-a-week session for thirty-five minutes. Frequency is more important than duration as we initiate this new habit. Gradually increase your time, working toward the goal of a minimum of thirteen minutes a day, the amount of time necessary to see permanent brain changes

Commit to a time of day that works best with your schedule. For most of us, that means first thing every morning. Perhaps ten to twenty minutes at lunchtime or after work are better for you. Some folks meditate right before bedtime. Just find a time that will work consistently with your unique responsibilities and duties.

The *Catechism* also acknowledges that "one cannot always meditate, but one can always enter into inner prayer, independently of the conditions of health, work, or emotional state."[110]

St. Francis de Sales was fully aware of the many distractions that come along with family life. Writing in the chapter "Of the Necessity of Prayer" (*Introduction to the Devout Life*, published in 1609), he says that "should it happen, through a pressure of business, or some accidental cause, that all your morning should pass away without allowing you leisure for this holy exercise of mental prayer . . . endeavor to repair this loss after dinner" (46). And throughout the day, "it is always necessary to rouse our minds to attentive recollection and consideration of the presence of God" (48).

PRACTICE

Bring your attention to your breath several times a day. This can be a simple form of prayer, too. Remember that "breath" and "spirit" are often translated as the same word in many languages. Focus on your breath, and continue bringing your attention back to it when your mind wanders.

Sixty years ago, the monk Thomas Merton was concerned about technology's ability to corrupt the human spirit. Of course, the gadgets and machines of his generation were vastly different from what we have today. He was fully aware of the blessings those machines imparted to humanity, like the improved farm equipment the monastery used to work the fields. He valued the benefits that advancements in technology could bring to human beings. But Merton cautioned that if we embraced technology uncritically, we might cease recognizing the spiritual dimension of life and forget about our neighbors. "There must be a renewal of communion between the traditional, contemplative disciplines and those of science, between the poet and the physicist, the priest and the depth-psychologist."[111]

Merton thought contemplation could be an antidote for this, saying meditation

is supposed to give you sufficient control over your mind and memory and will to enable you to recollect yourself and withdraw from exterior things and the business and activities and thoughts and concerns of temporal existence, and second—this is the real end of meditation—it teaches you how to become aware of the presence of God.[112]

If you do, your interior self will be awakened, as you'll begin to develop spiritual wonder, seeing the movements of grace in your life.

An additional concern of extended screen time among children is the marked decline of empathy among children of all ages.[113] Children simply cannot learn empathy and emotional intelligence from screens. It's a very slow-developing skill. We do not learn it through texting and emails. It's crucial to promote face-to-face interactions in meetings in our communities, churches, and schools, where everyone simply talks and shares. These opportunities boost the empathy skills of everyone involved.

The surges of dopamine every time we get a phone notification are quite addictive. An effective practice to thwart the overuse of cell phones is to nurture acts of kindness, which also release dopamine.

Instead of getting a dopamine hit from text messages, kids can practice empathic giving.

Strategies to Reduce Distractions and Interruptions

1. **Acknowledge that we are battling our information-seeking instinct.** Take a break from notifications, which means getting rid of all of the beeps, buzzes, and haptics, those vibrations

> For lack of attention, a thousand forms of loveliness elude us every day.
> —Evelyn Underhill

and tactile alerts. In the presence of a phone, our attention, focus, ability to solve problems, and logical thinking decrease. I followed this advice a while ago, and I'm here to report that I survived and have thrived. I no longer get interrupted by text messages, emails, or notifications. When I'm ready to take a break from a task, I glance at my phone or Gmail account to see if I need to reply to anyone. This "batching" of emails and text messages helps with efficiency, but also keeps the deleterious effects of distraction at bay. It is more effective than keeping a phone nearby and trying to suppress the desire to use it. As someone who regularly travels on airlines, I can report that it is the very best time to accomplish concentrated work. Why? Because with my phone off and earplugs in, there is almost no chance of interruptions at 35,000 feet in the air.

We are much better off if we nurture our concentration and attention muscles while discouraging any distractions. Remember the neuroscience: what we practice will grow neurons in our brains. If we stop a harmful practice, those neural connections associated with it will decrease.[114]

2. **Set up "no-phone zones."** When eating with friends and family, put your phone away. Just having a phone within earshot is distracting and takes up mental bandwidth. Studies show it also

reduces connection and conversation, thereby harming relationships. If you're talking to someone, for heaven's sake, put it away.
Keep it in your pocket when in line at the store, concert, or bank
if you aren't expecting an important text or email. Look around
and give your cognitive control a break. Take a few deep breaths
instead.

Figure out when and where you get sidetracked with scrolling.
When you eliminate the temptation by keeping your phone out
of reach and earshot, you'll make it easier to stay focused. Keep
your phone in your purse or glove compartment when driving,
taking it out for emergencies. In 2018, even the smartphone
makers acknowledged we should try to reduce our screen time.[115]

3. **Buy an alarm clock and leave your phone in the bathroom or
in another room.** Blue light from screens signals your brain to
wake up, and red light signals sleep. If you must use your phone
or computer at night, set the "night shift" tab in settings, or you
might try blue-light-blocking glasses or filters on your screen.
However, the jury is out about whether those devices actually
work:[116] The best solution is to try to minimize your exposure to
blue light a few hours before bedtime. You'll probably gain more
restful sleep and perhaps lessen eye strain or headaches.

4. **Take a social media break.** Many folks feel social media is taking a toll on their well-being. It might be difficult to walk away,
so commit to a temporary hiatus of a few weeks. That'll be easier
to consider, and at the end of that time, you might find that
quitting for good is pretty painless. I've talked to many who say
their lives are better after moving away from social media. Have a
real live conversation with your friend or family member instead
of posting a comment on Instagram or Facebook. Our time and
attention will be directed toward in-person or phone conversations, which are almost always more satisfying and deep.

5. **Monitor your daily use with your devices so you discover just how much of your day is spent looking at a screen.** It may be a revelation.

6. **Leave the phone/computer untouched for the first hour.** Have a cup of coffee, eat breakfast, shower, sit in prayer. In the evening, turn the phone off, allowing only emergency calls.

7. **Take a weekend "retreat" from tech.** See how you feel afterward. Our cell phones amaze in many ways, no question about it. But we can limit their deleterious effects by following a few of these simple suggestions. And then we will be able to fully appreciate the "thousand forms of loveliness" that surround us every day.

Because our jobs sometimes require us to respond immediately to emails, even at night and on weekends, we have a CPA problem. It's not an accounting issue, but an attention issue. Former Apple and Microsoft executive Linda Stone calls continuous partial attention (CPA) the phenomenon of always being alert and reachable, checking our screens frequently so we won't miss out on anything coming our way.[117] But living like this means we never fully pay attention to any one thing, as our brains continually scan for information. This leads to a lack of ability to focus on anything for very long.[118]

> So many of us have more and more information, and less and less time and space to make sense of it.
> —Pico Iyer

Apps to Nurture Our Spiritual Lives

It's pleasantly ironic that the very devices that can distract us also can help us. This is just a short list of apps that you can download and use.

- *Reimagining the Examen* from Loyola Press is an interactive app that leads you through a series of Examens, encouraging you to sit in prayer with God each day.

- "Centering Prayer": Guidelines for Centering, Opening Prayer, Beginning/ Ending Sound, Closing Prayer, etc. (Contemplative Outreach)
- "Pray As You Go" Fifteen-minute (or less) segments, with music, encouraging reflections. Also offers audio prayers, imaginative contemplation exercises, an audio rosary and stations of the cross, and an audio *examen.*
- "Sacred Space": Daily prayer, Scripture, actions, etc.
- Podcast: "The Examen with James Martin, SJ," https://examen.libsyn.com/
- Helpful meditation timers/background sounds: "Calm," "Insight Timer"

Admittedly, our smartphones come with innumerable and amazing features. But we cannot ignore that their use can negatively impact our brains in several ways. By adopting a few of these simple practices, we can lessen any cognitive impairments. I encourage you to incorporate some of these suggestions to maintain, and even improve, your attention and memory.

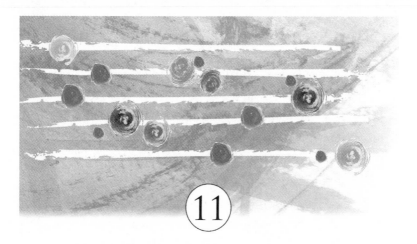

11

ALLOWING LEISURE
AND PLAY

*A lack of play should be treated like malnutrition—it's a health
risk to your body and mind.
Play is like fertilizer for brain growth. It's crazy not to use it.*
—STUART BROWN

It is a late September evening just before sunset, and I walk to our
porch and embark on a most important mission: listen to the crickets
and bask in the last light of day. It's still too early for bed, but after
a full day's work, it feels right to simply sit and observe: listen and
watch, note and experience this demarcation between day and night
before the stars appear and after our star, the sun, has set. This is not a
time for rushing, but a time for slowness and quiet. A time for thankfulness for another day, a time for exhaling. The fading light, muted
sounds, and escalating stillness combine to create a *thin place*, a Celtic
term. "Thin places are those rare locales where the distance between
Heaven and earth is compressed and you can sense the divine more
strongly."[119] It is a sacred space holding silence, one that is fertile and
timeless and fulsome. Others describe these locations as "the places in
the world where the walls are weak," where another dimension seems

nearer than usual and we experience our essential selves, perhaps even transcendence.

Who knew that leisure time can lead to transcendence? Yet it's surprising what might happen when we allow our-selves—not only at the end of the day but

> Have regular hours for work and play . . . then life will become a beautiful success.
> —Louisa May Alcott

at intervals throughout the day—to stop our work and relax, taking half an hour for tea or ten minutes to simply sit and be still.

Most of us spend our days "doing," moving from one task to the other, checking off each line on our to-do list. If we pose the question, "How are you?" to a friend or colleague, we often hear the answer "Busy!" It feels good to be accomplishing everything we've set out to do, but at other times, we're simply exhausted. We plow through the emails, the repetitive chores, the driving to and fro. This relentless pace is stressful, wearing us down physically and emotionally. I enjoy almost all my responsibilities but could do a little less and spend more time just being. That lesson hit home one night when I failed to notice—for half a day!—that my husband had substantially trimmed his scruffy beard (don't tell him I said that), a request I'd been making for a few months. I was so busy tending to my work list that his new look had gone unnoticed. So much for being present and attentive!

Rick Hanson, psychologist and author, recommends that we exam-ine our relationship to "doing." How can we do all the things we need to do without feeling stressed and pressed? First, he says, take care of the high-priority things and leave the small things behind. There's an old saying: "If you're filling a bucket, put in the big rocks first." Han-son also suggests engaging in activities freely and with a sense of ease. Take note when you feel pressed, and exhale slowly. Then you can con-tinue the doing, but with a sense of peace. Being mindful and realizing that we are pushing and pressing is key. We can take a step back and then just take on one thing at a time. Multitasking is a misnomer:

we are actually task switching, losing productivity with each switch. Focusing on one thing only will fill us with greater calm.

PRACTICE: FOR DURING THE DAY

Choose a cue from your daily environment as a prompt to check in with yourself: the phone ringing, a dog barking, the sound of an airplane overhead or a truck honking in the street. Ask yourself, "Am I pressing and anxious right now?" If that's true, it's time to take a breathing break. Close your eyes and breathe deeply for a minute or two, or stand up and stretch your arms and move your head in circles. My husband picks up his guitar and plays a short song to enjoy a break in his workday. Any of these will help you cultivate awareness.

Play is defined as a "pleasurable and apparently purposeless activity," or "anything spontaneously done for its own sake." Researchers have examined the relationships between having hobbies and our health, happiness, and quality of life. Studies indicate that people who spend more time in leisure activities have better overall health, including lower blood pressure and stress levels, less disease, and greater longevity. These folks sleep better, enjoy a wider circle of friends, and possess more meaning and fulfillment. Simply put, engaging in higher levels of leisure makes us happier. After seeing this, how can we not be energized to find more ways to get out and play? The very best form of play, from a psychological standpoint, is participation in team sports. But if that's not a realistic option, we simply need to find activities we enjoy that qualify as hobbies. To my chagrin, watching HGTV does not qualify! In fact, channel surfing may sound like a hobby, but it definitely does not constitute one. Hobbies should be purposeful, meaningful, and enjoyable activities. Passively watching TV does not usually qualify.[120]

PRACTICE

Take time to play with your child or grandchild. If you don't have a young family member nearby, volunteer to watch a friend's or a neighbor's child. Most parents will jump at the offer. Head to a playground or just bring a ball and bubbles. It doesn't take a big commitment: half an hour is good. And you don't simply watch but join in the play, which is quite different. When you toss the ball or blow bubbles, you are truly playing *with* rather than just watching. The child feels better, and so will you.

The importance of play cannot be overstated, and yet it is often the first proposed cut when school schedules need to be revised. Stuart Brown, the founder of the National Institute for Play, researches play and its contribution to healthy human development. He notes that when play is withheld from children, their ability to regulate emotions, express empathy, and trust companions is considerably narrowed.

When play is kept from laboratory rats, they fail to develop the ability to socialize normally or distinguish friend from foe. Play-deprived humans and animals become rigid, unable to respond to challenging situations and unexpected circumstances. They don't seek novelty and newness, which is essential to adapt and grow. Brown notes that adults who play very little become inflexible and depressed, unable to cope with the changing demands of the world around us.[121]

I grew up in a suburban St. Louis neighborhood with lots of kids around my age, and pickup games of all varieties were easy to initiate. Our backyard was a child's dream, with a seesaw and monkey bars flanking a large concrete slab that was wider than half of a basketball court. That court was the site of many games of "horse" and three-on-three basketball games. In winter, we transformed the concrete into an ice rink for informal hockey games. We also spent untold hours playing hotbox, Wiffle ball, and tag, and catching fireflies in our yard. This was where I first experienced "flow," the term coined by Mihaly Csik-szentmihalyi.[122] It occurs when we feel totally absorbed in an activity: energized, focused, and completely enjoying the moment, hardly sensing the passage of time. Numerous benefits are attributed to it, including increased productivity, creativity, learning, and confidence.

Another reason to encourage play, specifically play involving handwork, comes from a British study: surgeons report that many medical students are not able to perform surgeries as well as they should. Why? Because they have not honed their eye-hand coordination due to the lack of playing with origami, play dough, erector sets, yarn, sewing kits, LEGO sets, and so on. Physicians are recommending a return to the days of providing physical toys to boys and girls, where they learn to manipulate small pieces with their hands. All children—but particularly the next generation's knee surgeons, mechanics, and their clients—will benefit from better eye-hand coordination.

Many of us find that the first minutes upon waking are crucial for establishing a healthy trajectory for the hours ahead. Those initial moments hold the key to fashioning the day's vessel: will our vessel hold gratefulness, calm, and awareness? Or will we cradle hurry, worry, and scurry? Can we take in a few leisurely breaths and set the day's intention?

My daily routine begins with coffee brewing. I begin every day leisurely preparing just one cup of coffee. It's a ten-minute ritual, and I look forward to the entire process, which is very deliberate and uncomplicated. It provides a slow start to the day and time for me to be grateful for little things: clean water, electricity, food, my home, and all of life. The day begins unhurriedly, a luxury I don't take for granted.

It's interesting to know how coffee drinking affects our brains. First, we anticipate that cup of coffee, and our endocrine system creates and releases dopamine, known as the "anticipatory pleasure hormone." We start feeling good just knowing those first sips will be on our lips soon.

Second, because we associate coffee with pleasure, any actions we take that lead to drinking coffee release dopamine, too. As we brew coffee or walk to the coffee shop, more dopamine is released into our system.

Coffee's aroma, according to the journal of the American Chemical Society, "orchestrates the expression of more than a dozen genes and changes in protein expressions." The article goes on to say, "In other words, the saying 'wake up and smell the coffee' is more than just a metaphor."[123] Certain aromas trigger activity in the hippocampus, reminding us of past experiences and relationships. We smell coffee brewing and remember its effect on us.

And none of us needs to be reminded that coffee wakes us up. Caffeine reaches our brain only a few minutes after coffee crosses our lips. It blocks the action of adenosine, the hormone that causes us to feel sleepy. We feel more alert and lively. Because there is less adenosine in the body, glutamate is released, which increases our memory and learning capabilities. That's why we often focus and concentrate better after just one cup of coffee.[124]

PRACTICE

Every day this week, take a few moments upon waking to set an intention for the day. Brew your tea or coffee slowly, then take time to slowly drink it. Alternatively, you could bask in a leisurely breakfast. If I refuse to make room for these moments of appreciation and fulsome idleness, the work I do the rest of the day will be accomplished with less thoughtfulness and probably less skill.

I keep a cloth bookmark on my desk with the word *Balance* on it. It's there to remind me to ponder if I'm living in a balanced way. Do I say yes to too many opportunities? Merton warned us about the dangers of overcommitment and the desire to help everyone in everything. He calls it "violence," which may sound overly strong, but it's fairly accurate in both a spiritual and physical sense.

> To allow oneself to be carried away by a multitude of conflicting concerns, to surrender to too many demands, to commit oneself to too many projects, to want to help everyone in everything, is to succumb to violence.
>
> —Thomas Merton

We know that being too busy often begets stress. Research shows that the parts of the brain that control the stress response also play an important role in our susceptibility to inflammatory diseases such as arthritis. The areas of the brain associated with depression are the same as those of inflammatory diseases, so the two sometimes go hand in hand. We get sick and depressed when we are under too much stress for extended periods. Obviously, Merton was on to something decades before scientists proved his point.

One way to achieve balance and lessen our stress levels is to take regular moments to connect with ourselves, remembering who we want to be at our deepest level. Perhaps we go for a walk in nature, take a nap or a two-minute prayer break. The essential part is to honor your body's messages.

This message is clearly meant for me. I sometimes need to convince myself that I deserve a break and don't need to check another two or three items off my to-do list. Perhaps I should leisurely savor the day's simple gifts. As the fall unfolds, daylight decreases with the sun rising later and setting earlier. Pico Iyer tells us that this season's special lesson is to cherish everything, because it cannot last.[125] We can relish these days that remind us of how much we cannot afford to take for granted, how much there is to celebrate right now. The fading yellow and orange leaves bring an acute awareness that nothing lives forever. Perhaps in that awareness we snap out of our go-go-go mode and savor the beauty around us, take a few breaths, and treasure this day. The paperwork can wait, but today's gifts will be gone tomorrow.

We might think that we are able to appreciate leisure activities more after our work is completed. But a recent study shows that unearned fun is as enjoyable as fun "saved" for later, when all the day's chores are finished.[126] This research found that leisure activities are pleasurable regardless of when we experience them, even though we think we're going to feel guilty or distracted if we take a break before concluding our tasks. Because we are notoriously terrible at accurately predicting how we'll feel in the future, we forget what it's like to be immersed in leisure activities. We needn't wait until every item is checked off our to-do list before taking a break for an enjoyable diversion, even though it seems logical that "playing after working" would bring the greatest increase in joy. It makes no difference what comes first, work or play. The research is clear: Go enjoy yourself!

PRACTICE

Here are some suggestions to increase playtime. Call a friend to catch a movie, visit a museum, attend a concert or game, or hike on a nearby trail. Join a book club or a garden club. Invite friends over for game night. Explore the activities you enjoyed doing when you were ten years old. Are any of them accessible to you now? Did you play an instrument as a youngster? Can you pick it up again? Not only will that make you happier and healthier, but also your brain will thank you.

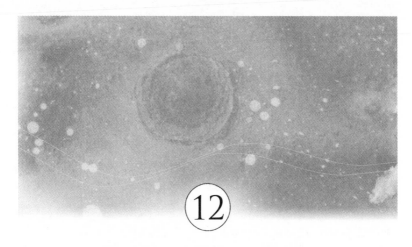

12

EXERCISES FOR BRAIN HEALTH

Do not wait; the time will never be "just right."
—NAPOLEON HILL

As we wind up our exploration of neuroscience and spiritual practices, I offer a list
of words and practices, from A to Z, that
will help us focus on nurturing our spiritual

> Of all ridiculous things, the
> most ridiculous seems to
> me, to be busy.
> —Søren Kierkegaard

lives and brain health. You might want to select one letter a week and
focus on that practice for seven days.

Attention. Take a seat in your yard or at a window and become aware
of the activity you see. Notice birds, insects, leaves, squirrels, trees,
flowers, bushes. Or, if you're a city dweller, notice people, the various
kinds of cars and buses, cyclists, dogs being walked, conversations taking place. Whatever is in your view, take note. Return the following
week, and the week after that, and just observe what has changed.

Beauty. Where do you find beauty? On your drive to work? In your
children's eyes? In *National Geographic* pictures? A beloved church

hymn? A piece of art? Take note of the many forms of beauty you encounter this week.

Create. Take a trip to a farmers' market or a health food store and buy an unfamiliar vegetable, grain, or spice. Consult a recipe book or the internet to create a dish with it. One of the benefits of signing up for a community-supported farm delivery is receiving less well-known items and learning to cook with them.

Dance. Dancing is great for the brain. A step class at your local gym qualifies as exercise *and* dance. You could also find a square dance in your city, which can be fun and energizing (and, for beginners, can also stimulate a lot of laughter, which is also good for you). Both are good for our brains and bodies, because when exercise is cognitively engaging, the benefit to our brain health is greater. If these activities don't suit your fancy, perhaps there's a dance club or drumming community nearby. Grab a friend and go.

Embrace. Hugs can boost immunity, lower stress, reduce depression, show appreciation, and increase self-esteem. They also release serotonin, a feel-good hormone, and oxytocin, another hormone that alleviates stress and promotes relaxation.[127]

Friends. Invite an acquaintance to join you for tea or coffee. Ask about their life, family, work, and hobbies to expand your connection. Scientists tell us that the more ties we have, both "weak" and "strong," the better our cognitive functioning and emotional and physical health will be. Even weak ties lessen the risk of mortality in later life.[128]

Garden. You use senses such as smell and touch when you garden, and your brain gets a workout: planning where and what to plant, how much sun is required, what colors will look best, and so on. Even planting a small window box of flowers is good for your brain.

Hobbies. Find a new hobby. Perhaps learn photography techniques or pottery or watercolor painting, all of which provide a workout for your brain and create new neural connections. Building LEGO sets with your children or grandchildren promotes sensory and spatial skills.

Improvise. Use your nondominant hand every which way you can: to brush your teeth, stir a pot, eat lunch, and open doors. You'll build lots of new connections in your brain.

Joke. Share jokes with friends or watch a few funny videos. Laughter really *is* the best medicine. It lowers stress, boosts immunity, decreases pain, and even helps prevent heart disease. The areas of the brain activated by humor are the same areas activated when we experience awe.[129]

Kindness. Being kind releases endorphins in the brain, which are natural painkillers. It improves our mood and lowers depression and anxiety. Kind people experience less stress and age more slowly than the average person.

Learn a language. Those who speak two languages have more gray and white matter in the brain. From age twenty-five, our brain function begins to decline. But a bilingual brain suffers much less steep declines in memory, efficiency, and processing speed, perhaps even keeping Alzheimer's at bay.[130]

Meditate. Stilling the mind and breathing deeply alter structures in the brain, allowing us to handle stress better. Meditation increases thickness in the hippocampus, which controls memory and learning, while improving focus and concentration. Research suggests that meditators' brains experience less atrophy in both white and gray matter, meaning their brains work more like the brains of people decades younger.

Nature. Being in nature has a positive impact on our brains and moods. Natural environments reduce stress and cortisol while increasing our attention, creativity, and social interactions. Impoverished neighborhoods with green spaces experience less violence and crime and more civility compared to those lacking such greenery.[131]

Observe. Try observing everything around you with loving eyes. Our brains possess a negativity bias, as we've evolved to pay attention to difficulty, danger, and problems. Being aware of this bias can help us switch to a more gentle, caring gaze. If we observe each person as unique and precious, made in God's image, people will sense our warmth and compassion, and we may find that friendliness radiating back to us.

> If I had my life to live over again, I would ask that not a thing be changed, but that my eyes be opened wider.
> —Jules Renard

Pray and play. One simple and effective prayer is the Daily Examen, often done in the evening, where you review how God was active in your day. As we practice noticing how God was present with us throughout the day, we prime our brains to cultivate a contemplative stance in all we do. It's a simple, easy, and effective practice that reduces stress levels and fosters better sleep and heart health.

Dr. Rae Jean Proeschold-Bell, associate research professor at Duke University, spoke with me in November 2019 about her research on the Daily Examen. She found that clergy who prayed the Daily Examen saw decreases in stress and anxiety and increases in their heart rate variability (HRV). (HRV is the amount of time between heartbeats. Healthy hearts have more variability between each beat.) She concluded that praying the Daily Examen is not only good for the soul; it's good for the heart, mind, and body.

Challenging games can help prevent declines in memory and improve brain function. Chess, word puzzles, Fibbage (a family favorite in the online Jackbox Games), and other social games help ward off stress and depression, too.[132]

Quotidian. The daily, ordinary experience of life is extraordinary if only we take a moment to think about it. The sun comes up in the morning, the stars appear at night, and millions of little miracles occur in between those daily events. Truly, just to be here is incredible. As Emily Dickinson said, "To live is so startling it leaves little time for anything else."

Recharge. Your prefrontal cortex (or PFC) in the brain works hard because it's responsible for maintaining focus and willpower and thinking logically, among other duties. Studies show that taking a break every seventy-five to ninety minutes restores motivation, increases creativity and productivity, and improves memory formation.[133]

Smell. The next time you bring home fresh produce, pick up some of the items and smell them. Our modern world of plastic packaging and deodorized objects minimizes opportunities to develop our olfactory system. With a small amount of practice, however, we can increase our ability to distinguish scents and build neural connections in the "smell" area of our brains.

Travel. Many of us love to travel, and it's also great for our brains. Novel sights, sounds, smells, foods, roads, languages, and customs put our brains on high alert (in a good way), and stimulate new connections in our brains. We live more in the present moment because everything is new, lessening stress and anxiety.

Unique you. The more we recognize our uniqueness, the more we exercise regularly, eat healthfully, and tend to friendships, all of which are essential for optimal brain health. Furthermore, affirmations activate the reward circuits of our brains, decreasing perceived pain and helping us handle the stresses of life.[134] Take a moment now and acknowledge two or three unique traits you possess, perhaps ones that others have mentioned in conversation. Jot them down and keep in a handy location. Review the list when you need some encouragement.

Remember the positive impact of positive self-talk on your confidence, resilience, and stress.

Volunteer. Volunteering engages your mind and body in many ways. Meeting new people can boost the feel-good neurochemicals of oxytocin, serotonin, dopamine, and endorphins. These reduce stress and anxiety, improve your immune system, and increase overall well-being. Volunteering may also reduce the risk of dementia and Alzheimer's disease.[135]

Walk. Invite a friend, neighbor, or coworker to take a walk on an unfamiliar path. Walking will encourage your brain to release endorphins, boosting your mental health and happiness while lowering your sensitivity to stress and pain.

eXhale. Several times a day, practice inhaling to the count of four, exhaling to the count of six. Taking longer to exhale relaxes the nervous system and brings calm to the present moment. When we inhale, our heart rate speeds up. When we exhale, our heart rate decreases, releasing tension and agitation.

> The whole world is a series of miracles, but we're so used to them that we call them everyday things.
> —Hans Christian Andersen

Young at heart. Reconnect with a childhood activity or try one you always wished you had learned long ago. It could be as simple as reading a comic book, finger painting, jumping on a pogo stick, coloring a page, drawing with chalk, riding a bike, roller skating, or swinging on a park swing. If you need some ideas, go to your local craft store and head to the children's section.

Z's. Aim for seven to eight hours of sleep per night to promote learning, creativity, focus, memory, and overall health. Proper sleep helps maintain your ideal blood pressure, blood sugar levels, and weight, while keeping your immune system healthy. Getting adequate sleep also means you'll be less likely to become depressed or anxious.[136]

Hopefully, you've come to these last pages with new tools to "put into practice what light you already have." I hope you feel more equipped and motivated to nourish

> Embrace the present moment as an ever-flowing source of holiness.
> —Jean-Pierre de Caussade

your light and share it with those in your community, workplace, family, and church. Try a few practices to discover ones that are a good fit for you. Be patient with yourself. Remember to take a few deep breaths throughout your day, connecting your spirit to God's abiding presence.

Your unique light is needed in our world. May the lessons found here support and inspire your journey. I wish you abundant blessings!

ACKNOWLEDGMENTS

So many people provided support and advice during the creation of this book. My thanks to the Loyola Press family, particularly Carol Dreps and Joellyn Cicciarelli, for their generosity and encouragement. A deep bow of gratitude to Maria Cuadrado for her reassurances during the writing process, to Vinita Wright for her professional guidance and editing, and to Carrie Freyer and Gary Jansen for their genuine enthusiasm. Heartfelt appreciation also goes to Mike Leach, accomplished writer and editor, who has inspired me with his guidance, wisdom, and joy.

Too numerous to list are friends, mentors, coworkers, customers, and retreatants who have generously affirmed my work, listened patiently, offered suggestions, and provided kind feedback. I owe a debt of gratitude to all of them.

To our children, Sarah, Elizabeth, and Jackson: I am so proud of the young adults you have become. Thanks for providing plenty of stories to share with others!

To our grandchildren Morgan, Percy, Milly, Sawyer, Mack, and Charlie: the joy and playfulness you bring into our lives is immeasurable. I can't wait to see what adventures lie ahead for all of us!

Finally, I do very little without the love and encouragement of my husband, Jack. He is my sounding board, IT guy, and partner of forty years. How many times I asked, "Can I read this to you and get your feedback?" and he thoughtfully pondered my question. As George Eliot said, "What greater thing is there for two human souls than to feel that they are joined for life—to strengthen each other in all labor, to rest on each other in all sorrow, to minister to each other . . .?"

ENDNOTES

1. Aldous Huxley. *The Perennial Philosophy*. (New York: Harper & Brothers, 1945), 285.

2. https://www.vatican.va/archive/ccc_css/archive/catechism/p4s1c3a1.htm

3. Richard H. Schmidt, *God Seekers: Twenty Centuries of Christian Spiritualities* (Grand Rapids: Wm. B. Eerdmans, 2008), 215.

4. Matthew A. Killingsworth and Daniel T. Gilbert, "A Wandering Mind Is an Unhappy Mind," *Science* 330, no. 6006 (November 12, 2010): 932.

5. Killingsworth and Gilbert, "A Wandering Mind," 932.

6. Herbert Benson, MD, with Miriam Z. Klipper, *The Relaxation Response* (New York: Avon, 1976 reissue).

7. Guido P. H. Band and Roderick J. S. Gerritsen, "Breath of Life: The Respiratory Vagal Stimulation Model of Contemplative Activity," *Frontiers in Human Neuroscience* 12 (October 9, 2018), 397, https://www.ncbi.nlm.nih.gov/pmc/articles/PMC6189422/.

8. https://www.sciencedaily.com/releases/2018/05/180510101254.htm.

9. Brother Lawrence of the Resurrection, OCD, *Writings and Conversations on the Practice of the Presence of God*, trans. Salvatore Sciurba (Washington, DC: ICS Publications, 1994), 116.

10. *Writings and Conversations on the Practice of the Presence of God*, xxxiv.

11. Teresa of Avila, *Foundations*, 5,8.

12. Ronald Siegel, PsyD, "Tailoring Practices to Fit Changing Needs," lecture 8, *The Science of Mindfulness: A Research-Based Path to Well-Being* (Chantilly, VA: The Great Courses, 2014), DVD.

13. Denis Larrivee and Luis Echarte, "Contemplative Meditation and Neuroscience: Prospects for Mental Health," *Journal of Religion and Health* 57, no. 3 (2018), 964.

14. Ellen J. Langer, *Mindfulness* (Reading, MA: Addison-Wesley, 1989).

15. https://www.medicalnewstoday.com/articles/327310.

16. *Practice of the Presence of God*, 65.

17. Thomas Merton, *The Wisdom of the Desert* (New York: New Directions, 1960).

18. Thomas Merton, *Seeds of Contemplation* (London: Burns and Oates, 1962).

19. Kim Nataraja, *Journey to the Heart: Christian Contemplation through the Centuries*, 2011, 378.

20. W. C. Compton and Edward Hoffman, *Positive Psychology: The Science of Happiness and Flourishing*, 2nd ed. (Belmont, CA: Thompson Wadsworth, 2013).

21. J. Finley, *Christian Meditation: Experiencing the Presence of God*, New York: Harper Collins, 2004, 46–47.

22. Finley, 50.

23. E. Kadloubovsky and G. E. H. Palmer, *Early Fathers from the Philokalia* (London: Faber & Faber, 1971), 161.

24. Elizabeth Blackburn and Elissa Epel, *The Telomere Effect* (New York: Grand Central Publishing [Hachette Book Group], 2017).

25. Kevin King, et al., "Effect of Leukocyte Telomere Length on Total and Regional Brain Volumes in a Large Population-Based Cohort," *JAMA Neurology* 71, no. 10 (2014): 1247–54.

26. Blackburn and Epel, *The Telomere Effect*, 29–35.

27. Blackburn and Epel, *The Telomere Effect*, 156.

28. Goleman and Davidson, *Altered Traits*, 273.

29. Adam Gazzaley and Larry D. Rosen, *The Distracted Mind: Ancient Brains in a High-Tech World* (Cambridge, MA: MIT Press, 2016), 190.

30. Tom Ireland, "What Does Mindfulness Meditation Do to Your Brain?" *Scientific American* (guest blog), June 12, 2014, https://blogs.scientificamerican.com/guest-blog/what-does-mindfulness-meditation-do-to-your-brain/.

31. Kathleen A. Garrison et al., "Meditation Leads to Reduced Default Mode Network Activity Beyond an Active Task," *Cognitive, Affective, and Behavioral Neuroscience* 15, no. 3 (September 2015): 712–20.

32. Goleman and Davidson, *Altered Traits*, 252–53.

33. Julia C. Basso et al., "Brief, Daily Meditation Enhances Attention, Memory, Mood, and Emotional Regulation in Non-Experienced Meditators." Abstract. *Behavioural Brain Research*, 356 (January 1, 2019), 208–20.

34. Adam Gazzaley and Larry D. Rosen, *The Distracted Mind: Ancient Brains in a High-Tech World* (Cambridge, MA: MIT Press, 2016), 84–88.

35. https://scholar.harvard.edu/sara_lazar/home.

36. https://pubmed.ncbi.nlm.nih.gov/
26445019/?from_term=alzheimers+and+meditation&from_pos=1
https://www.medicalnewstoday.com/articles/
323722#Changes-in-beta-amyloid-and-symptoms

37. https://thriveglobal.com/stories/
how-gratitude-actually-changes-your-brain-and-is-good-for-business/.

38. R. McCraty et al., "The Impact of a New Emotional Self-Management Program on Stress, Emotions, Heart Rate Variability, DHEA and Cortisol," Abstract. *Integrative Physiological and Behavioral Science* 33 no. 2 (April–June 1998), 151–70. Study published by the National Center for Biotechnology Information. (Dehydroepiandrosterone, or DHEA, helps produce other hormones.)

39. https://www.ncbi.nlm.nih.gov/pubmed/28698643. Abstract.

40. Robert A. Emmons and Michael E. McCullough, "Counting Blessings versus Burdens: An Experimental Investigation of Gratitude and Subjective Well-Being in Daily Life," *Journal of Personality and Social Psychology* 84, no. 2 (2003): 377–89, https://greatergood.berkeley.edu/images/application_uploads/
Emmons-CountingBlessings.pdf.

41. https://greatergood.berkeley.edu/images/application_uploads/
Wood-GratitudeSleep.pdf.

42. https://www.tandfonline.com/doi/abs/10.1080/17439760.2020.1716054

43. Summer Allen, PhD, *The Science of Gratitude White Paper*, Greater Good Science Center (May 2018), https://ggsc.berkeley.edu/images/uploads/
GGSC-JTF_White_Paper-Gratitude-FINAL.pdf.

44. David DeSteno, *Emotional Success: The Power of Gratitude, Compassion, and Pride* (New York: Houghton Mifflin Harcourt, 2018) https://www.inc.com/
geoffrey-james/
neuroscience-says-your-body-mind-get-stronger-when-you-focus-on-this-one-thingdr
aft-1562273865.html.

45. Sonja Lyubomirsky, *The How of Happiness: A Scientific Approach to Getting the Life You Want* (New York: Penguin Press, 2008), 275.

46. Lyubomirsky, *The How of Happiness*, 267.

47. Clara Strauss et al., "What Is Compassion and How Can We Measure It? A Review of Definitions and Measures," Abstract. https://www.ncbi.nlm.nih.gov/pubmed/27267346.

48. McNeill, Morrison, and Nouwen, *Compassion: A Reflection on the Christian Life.* (Garden City, N.Y: Image Books, 1983), 3–4.

49. "Why You Should Pay Attention to Chronic Inflammation" (October 14, 2014), https://health.clevelandclinic.org/why-you-should-pay-attention-to-chronic-inflammation/.

50. https://www.webmd.com/heart/news/20130614/volunteering-may-be-good-for-the-heart-in-more-ways-than-one

51. Emma Seppala, Timothy Rossomando, and James R. Doty, "Social Connection and Compassion: Important Predictors of Health and Well-Being," *Social Research* 80, no. 2 (Summer 2013): 411–430, http://www.ccare.stanford.edu/article/social-connection-and-compassion-important-predictors-of-health-and-well-being/.

52. https://www.sciencedirect.com/science/article/abs/pii/S0306453009001991.

53. https://www.mindful.org/three-powerful-mindfulness-practices-try-road/.

54. Danusha Laméris, *Bonfire Opera* (Pittsburgh: University of Pittsburgh Press, 2020), 83. https://voxpopulisphere.com/2019/08/11/danusha-lameris-small-kindnesses/.

55. https://www.ncbi.nlm.nih.gov/pmc/articles/PMC4941164/

56. https://www.psychologytoday.com/us/blog/cutting-edge-leadership/201206/there-s-magic-in-your-smile. Also https://www.psychologytoday.com/us/blog/changepower/201605/the-9-superpowers-your-smile.

57. https://www.nytimes.com/2019/04/18/well/mind/can-botox-and-cosmetic-surgery-chill-our-relationships-with-others.html.

58. Jules Masserman, Stanley Wechkin, and William Terris, "'Altruistic' Behavior in Rhesus Monkeys," *American Journal of Psychiatry* (1964). No online access.

59. Roman Krznaric, *Empathy: What It Is and How to Get It* (New York: Penguin Random House, 2014), 24.

60. Krznaric, *Empathy*, 131–32.

61. https://pubmed.ncbi.nlm.nih.gov/20688954/

62. Sara B. Algoe and Jonathan Haidt, "Witnessing Excellence in Action: The Other-Praising Emotions of Elevation, Gratitude, and Admiration," Abstract. *Journal of Positive Psychology*, 4 no. 2 (2009): 105–127, https://www.ncbi.nlm.nih.gov/pmc/articles/PMC2689844/.

63. Jessica Cerretani, "The Contagion of Happiness," *Harvard Medicine* (Winter 2020), https://hms.harvard.edu/magazine/science-emotion/contagion-happiness.

64. Lyubomirsky, *The How of Happiness*, 133.

65. Julia Cameron, *The Artist's Way: The Spiritual Path to Higher Creativity*, 25th anniversary edition (New York: Penguin, 2016), 20.

66. Christopher K. Germer, *The Mindful Path to Self-Compassion* (New York: The Guilford Press, 2009), 2.

67. Kristen Neff, *Self-Compassion* (New York: Harper Collins, 2011).

68. https://www.psychologicalscience.org/news/ why-you-should-stop-being-so-hard-on-yourself.html.

69. Christopher K. Germer, *The Mindful Path to Self-Compassion* (New York: The Guilford Press, 2009.)

70. https://www.ncbi.nlm.nih.gov/pmc/articles/PMC3890922/.

71. https://positivepsychology.com/positive-self-talk/

72. https://www.psychologicalscience.org/news/releases/compassion-training.html.

73. Rob Walker, *The Art of Noticing: 131 Ways to Spark Creativity, Find Inspiration, and Discover Joy in the Everyday* (New York: Alfred A. Knopf, 2019).

74. Oliver Sacks, "Why We Need Gardens" in *Everything in Its Place* (New York: Alfred A. Knopf, 2019), 243.

75. Mary Carol Hunter, Brenda W. Gillespie, and Sophie Yu-Pu Chen, "Urban Nature Experiences Reduce Stress in the Context of Daily Life Based on Salivary Biomarkers," *Frontiers in Psychology* (April 4, 2019), https://www.frontiersin.org/ articles/10.3389/fpsyg.2019.00722/full.

76. "Seeing Greenery Linked to Less Intense and Frequent Cravings," Abstract. *Neuroscience News*, (July 12, 2019), https://neurosciencenews.com/ green-space-cravings-14468/.

77. Ellen J. Langer. *Mindfulness*. Reading, MA: Addison-Wesley, 1989.

78. https://www.researchgate.net/publication/309537908/.

79. https://neurosciencenews.com/nature-health-wellbeing-14233/.

80. https://www.ncbi.nlm.nih.gov/pmc/articles/PMC4929355/

81. https://greatergood.berkeley.edu/article/item/
    why_is_nature_so_good_for_your_mental_health.

82. Dacher Keltner and Jonathan Haidt, "Approaching Awe, a Moral, Spiritual, and
    Aesthetic Emotion," *Cognition and Emotion* 17 (March 2003): 297–314.

83. Carolyn Gregoire "How Awe-Inspiring Experiences Can Make You Happier, Less
    Stressed, and More Creative" *HuffPost*, September 22, 2014 (updated December
    6, 2017) https://www.huffpost.com/entry/the-psychology-of-awe_n_5799850.

84. The Christophers, *Better to Light One Candle* (New York: Continuum,
    2000) 210.

85. "Can Creativity Be Taught?," https://www.creativityatwork.com/2012/03/23/
    can-creativity-be-taught/.

86. https://www.inc.com/magazine/201402/ryan-underwood/
    creativity-boosters-neuroscience.html.

87. Wallace J. Nichols, *Blue Mind: The Surprising Science That Shows How Being
    Near, In, On, or Under Water Can Make You Happier, Healthier, More Connected,
    and Better at What You Do* (New York: Little, Brown, 2014).

88. https://www.ncbi.nlm.nih.gov/pubmed/26284745.

89. https://www.huffpost.com/entry/
    baking-for-others-psychology_n_58dd0b85e4b0e6ac7092aaf8 and
    https://www.guideposts.org/better-living/positive-living/
    emotional-and-mental-health/the-psychological-benefits-of-baking-for-others

90. https://www.guideposts.org/better-living/positive-living/
    emotional-and-mental-health/the-psychological-benefits-of-baking-for-others.

91. https://www.huffpost.com/entry/
    baking-for-others-psychology_n_58dd0b85e4b0e6ac7092aaf8?ncid=APPLENEWS0
    0001.

92. https://www.linkedin.com/pulse/
    theres-limit-your-creativity-definition-either-judy-pindroh-pretto/.

93. https://www.nielsen.com/us/en/insights/news/2018/
    time-flies-us-adults-now-spend-nearly-half-a-day-interacting-with-media.html.

94. Adam Gazzaley and Larry D. Rosen, *The Distracted Mind: Ancient Brains in a
    High-Tech World* (Cambridge, MA: MIT Press, 2016), 123–126.

95. https://www.psychologytoday.com/us/basics/attention

96. Daniel Goleman and Richard J. Davidson, *Altered Traits: Science Reveals How
    Meditation Changes Your Mind, Brain, and Body* (New York: Penguin, 2017).

97. Goleman and Davidson, *Altered Traits*, 138.

98. Gazzaley and Rosen, *The Distracted Mind*, 78.

99. https://www.memory-key.com/research/news/
how-cognitive-reserve-helps-protect-seniors-cognitive-decline and
https://www.rd.com/health/wellness/how-the-brain-benefits-with-aging/.

100. https://www.nytimes.com/2019/03/26/smarter-living/
stop-letting-modern-distractions-steal-your-attention.html.

101. https://www.apa.org/news/press/releases/2017/02/checking-devices

102. https://www.nytimes.com/2019/03/26/smarter-living/
stop-letting-modern-distractions-steal-your-attention.html.

103. https://www.health.harvard.edu/mind-and-mood/
sour-mood-getting-you-down-get-back-to-nature.

104. Marc G. Berman, John Jonides, and Stephen Kaplan, "The Cognitive Benefits
of Interacting with Nature," *Psychological Science* 19 (December 2008): 1207–12.

105. https://www.health.harvard.edu/mind-and-mood/
sour-mood-getting-you-down-get-back-to-nature.

106. https://pubmed.ncbi.nlm.nih.gov/20074458/

107. Goleman and Davidson, *Altered Traits*, 251.

108. Goleman and Davidson, *Altered Traits*, 181.

109. https://www.ncbi.nlm.nih.gov/pubmed/26445019 and
https://www.beingpatient.com/meditation-cognitive-decline/.

110. *Catechism of the Catholic Church*, no. 2710, https://www.vatican.va/archive/
ccc_css/archive/catechism/p4s1c3a1.htm.

111. Paul R. Dekar, *Thomas Merton: Twentieth-Century Wisdom for
Twenty-First-Century Living* (Eugene, OR: Cascade Books, 2011), 108.
http://merton.org/ITMS/Annual/17/Dekar216-234.pdf)

112. Thomas Merton, *New Seeds of Contemplation* (New Directions Publishing,
1972), 217.

113. https://emerj.com/ai-podcast-interviews/
snuggle-up-with-technology-but-dont-leave-empathy-in-the-cold-a-conversation-with
-dr-sherry-turkle/.

114. https://www.nytimes.com/2019/03/26/smarter-living/
stop-letting-modern-distractions-steal-your-attention.html.

115. https://www.nytimes.com/2019/04/01/smarter-living/
how-to-make-your-phone-limit-your-screen-time-for-you.html

116. https://www.webmd.com/eye-health/news/20191216/do-blue-light-glasses-work.

117. https://www.researchgate.net/publication/
235340722_Multitasking_or_Continuous_Partial_Attention_A_Critical_Bottleneck
_for_Digital_Natives

118. https://www.nytimes.com/2019/03/26/smarter-living/
stop-letting-modern-distractions-steal-your-attention.html.

119. Eric Weiner, *Man Seeks God: My Flirtations with the Divine* (New York:
Hachette, 2011), 66.

120. Tara Parker-Pope, "How to Find a Hobby," *New York Times*,
https://www.nytimes.com/guides/smarterliving/how-to-find-a-hobby.

121. https://onbeing.org/programs/stuart-brown-play-spirit-and-character/.

122. Mihaly Csikszentmihalyi, *Flow: The Psychology of Optimal Experience* (New
York: HarperCollins, 1990).

123. https://www.inc.com/geoffrey-james/
your-first-cup-of-coffee-does-these-5-surprising-things-for-your-brain-each-every-day.
html.

124. https://www.inc.com/geoffrey-james/
your-first-cup-of-coffee-does-these-5-surprising-things-for-your-brain-each-every-day.
html.

125. https://www.nytimes.com/2019/09/20/opinion/
aging-marriage-autumn.html?searchResultPosition=1.

126. https://neurosciencenews.com/unearned-fun-psychology-6936/.

127. https://www.thehealthy.com/mental-health/benefits-of-hugging/.

128. https://www.washingtonpost.com/national/health-science/
how-casual-daily-interactions-protect-your-health/2018/07/06/
fc62a468-4e33-11e8-84a0-458a1aa9ac0a_story.html.

129. https://www.helpguide.org/articles/mental-health/laughter-is-the-best-medicine.htm.
Also Michelle Boston, "How Being Funny Changes Your Brain," *USC News*,
February 24, 2017, https://news.usc.edu/116675/
studying-creativity-and-the-brain-is-no-joke/.

130. Ramin Skibba, "Speaking Two Languages May Help the Aging Brain,"
Washington Post, December 8, 2018, https://www.washingtonpost.com/national/

health-science/speaking-two-languages-may-help-the-aging-brain/2018/12/07/
f93489c8-f8b0-11e8-8d64-4e79db33382f_story.html.

131. Kristophe Green and Dacher Keltner, "What Happens When We Reconnect
with Nature," The Greater Good Science Center at the University of California,
Berkeley, March 1, 2017, https://greatergood.berkeley.edu/article/item/
what_happens_when_we_reconnect_with_nature. Also, Harvard Men's Health
Watch, "Sour Mood Getting You Down? Get Back to Nature," July 2018,
https://www.health.harvard.edu/mind-and-mood/
sour-mood-getting-you-down-get-back-to-nature.

132. Lawrence Robinson, Melinda Smith, MA, Jeanne Segal and Jennifer Shubin,
"The Benefits of Play for Adults" HelpGuide, June 2019,
https://www.helpguide.org/articles/mental-health/benefits-of-play-for-adults.htm.

133. "Want to Be More Productive in 2018? Take More Breaks" MIT Sloan
Executive Education Blog, December 3, 2017, https://executive.mit.edu/blog/
want-to-be-more-productive-in-2018-take-more-breaks. Also, Meg Selig, "How Do
Work Breaks Help Your Brain? 5 Surprising Answers," Change Power (blog),
Psychology Today, April 18, 2017, https://www.psychologytoday.com/us/blog/
changepower/201704/how-do-work-breaks-help-your-brain-5-surprising-answers.

134. Debbie Hampton, "The Neuroscience of How Affirmations Help Your Mental
Health," The Best Brain Possible (blog), December 22, 2019,
https://thebestbrainpossible.com/affirmations-brain-depression-anxiety/.

135. "Do Your Brain a Favor—Volunteer," Alzheimer Society Canada, October 1,
2018, https://alzheimer.ca/en/Home/About-dementia/Brain-health/
Volunteering-tips.

136. "Surprising Reasons to Get More Sleep," WebMD, June 18, 2019,
https://www.webmd.com/sleep-disorders/benefits-sleep-more#1.

ABOUT THE AUTHOR

Anne Kertz Kernion, founder of the inspirational greeting card company Cards by Anne, is an international lecturer and retreat leader and holds an MA in theology from Duquesne University and a B.S. in environmental engineering from Penn State University. She is a former adjunct faculty member at Carlow University and author of *A Year of Spiritual Companionship*. Anne teaches yoga and enjoys biking and hiking. She and her husband, Jack, have three grown children and six grandchildren.

More Reading on Spiritual Wellness

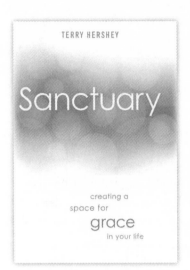

SANCTUARY
CREATING A SPACE FOR GRACE IN YOUR LIFE

TERRY HERSHEY

Sanctuary not only defines what sanctuary is but why we need it, where we can find it, and how we can create it as space and habit. The challenge of daily life takes a lot of energy, time, and effort. Join Terry Hershey as he guides you towards creating a way of daily life that helps you reflect, refresh, and recharge.

Hardcover I 978-0-8294-4264-9 I $22.95
Paperback I 978-0-8294-4357-8 I $16.95

THE POWER OF PAUSE
BECOMING MORE BY DOING LESS

TERRY HERSHEY

Using stories, meditations, inspirational quotes, and calls-to-action in each chapter, Terry Hershey's *The Power of Pause* will help anyone learn how to slow down, take back the life God intended for you, and experience life to its fullest.

Hardcover I 978-0-8294-2862-9 I $16.95
Paperback I 978-0-8294-3546-7 I $12.95

If you're interested in sharing *The Power of Pause* for a group workshop or retreat, checkout *Becoming More by Doing Less: Practicing the Power of Pause.*

DVD I 978-0-8294-3116-2 I $19.95

To Order:
Call **800.621.1008**, visit **store.loyolapress.com**, or visit your local bookseller.

More Reading on Spiritual Wellness

7 KEYS TO SPIRITUAL WELLNESS
ENRICHING YOUR FAITH BY STRENGTHENING THE HEALTH OF YOUR SOUL

JOE PAPROCKI

Just as with our physical wellness, there are important strategies for maintaining our spiritual wellness. To help readers evaluate the status of their "spiritual immune system" and achieve spiritual wellness, best-selling author and renowned speaker Joe Paprocki provides 7 enduring and reliable strategies that you can integrate into daily life. At its core, this book will help you see Christian faith as a spiritual path towards a life of spiritual wellness and meaning.

Paperback | 978-0-8294-3689-1 | $12.95

MICROSHIFTS
TRANSFORMING YOUR LIFE ONE STEP AT A TIME

GARY JANSEN

Does a plan for a lifestyle change feel overwhelming? Well, Gary Jansen provides a practical strategy that uses many little changes for big improvements to physical, mental, and spiritual wellness. *MicroShifts* is Jansen's guide of over 40 *microshifts* you can make, starting today, as well as a **28-Day MicroShift Challenge** to transform your life.

Paperback | 978-0-8294-4536-7 | $14.95